Bert Jones has done all the hard work of panning for gold in his *Leadership Journal*. In it you will only find large and precious nuggets of leadership advice that will be of inestimable value to you on your leadership journey. Read it to find these treasures!

David Stevens, MD
CEO Emeritus
Christian Medical & Dental Associations

Bert Jones has captured years of leadership insights in a small volume that I found relevant and helpful. In fact, it's useful not only to the medical community but to anyone who cares about leading well. Bert is both perceptive and practical, and his journal is digestible. You can use what you read instantly. I recommend it highly.

Dr. Tim Elmore
CEO and Founder, Growing Leaders

There are two ways one can grow as a leader: your own experience and the experience of others. Both ways are necessary, but too few leaders take time to make the most of the experience of others. This book brings a true leader's lifetime of experience to anyone willing to listen, learn, and grow from it.

Chad Hall, DMin, MCC
President, Coach Approach Ministries

When you know the author of a book, you lean in very carefully to take in the wisdom of the author. But when you have *watched* the author practice what he or she is writing about and you see the authenticity, then you bathe yourself in the wisdom! I found myself doing just that. These journaled snapshots of leadership wisdom are rich. Gems such as, "Bigger is not better; better is better" and, "The works of leadership far outweigh the perks of leadership" are not just catchy but are refreshingly true.

Dr. Barbara K. Bellefeuille
President, Bethel University

Bert Jones is a lifelong student of leadership. He is also an extraordinary pastor and teacher who has talent to both challenge and encourage his listeners. The insights contained in his leadership journal read like notes of the best lessons found over his thirty-three years of diligent research. Not just platitudes, this work contains applications to help you become a better leader today and tomorrow.

Dr. Lisle Whitman
Board of Trustees President
Christian Medical & Dental Associations

We are all leaders in our spheres of influence. To lead well, we must continue to grow and improve— or as Bert says, "yearn to learn." What a gift Bert Jones has given us by sharing the insights he has learned on his leadership journey. Bert definitely has a way with words. In his preaching, teaching, and writing, with alliteration, analogies, and other masterful uses of English, he brings his message home in a short, memorable form. Don't be deceived by the length of this book. Each succinct point he makes is loaded with content and gives food for thought. You can spend quite a while pondering and applying these principles. It is rich. The lessons from Rev. Jones' journey can make each of our journeys more productive and more glorifying to God.

Gloria Halverson, MD
Past President and Board of Trustees Chair
Christian Medical & Dental Associations

A literal gold mine of timeless treasures for becoming an even better leader while coaching those around and behind you to excellence in all they do.

Walt Larimore, MD
Best-Selling Author of *At First Light: A True World War II Story of a Hero, His Bravery, and an Amazing Horse*

Once again, Bert Jones delivers with timeless wisdom and practical leadership advice in this one-of-a-kind journal. Whether you are young in your career or an experienced professional, this journal will help you navigate daily challenges and decisions while allowing for reflection and personal growth. Journaling has always helped me expand my self-awareness and has been a critical development tool as an executive. This journal, with its numerous leadership pearls, is sure to become a must-have for executives serious about growing their leadership acumen.

Eric S. Edwards, MD, PhD
Co-Founder and Chief Executive Officer
Phlow Corporation

This will be one of those "read every year" resources for leaders due to the depth and scope of the content and the book's leader-friendly format. Bert Jones has crafted a book for leaders by a leader who clearly understands the leadership journey you and I are on. Loaded with biblical and practical insights, coaching, and encouragement, this book will help us faithfully fulfill the mission God has given us.

Terry Linhart, PhD
Founder and Director of Arbor Research Group
Author of *The Self-Aware Leader*

Bert has been cultivating a culture of leadership for over thirty-three years. This book draws on both his invaluable experience and lessons learned during that time. This is a perfect resource for my team and future leaders. As a leader and a parent, I see this as a fantastic resource to use as I develop next-generation leaders in my home.

Dan Book
Vice President, Sales and Agency Operations
Brotherhood Mutual Insurance Company

I've read dozens of leadership books. This one is special as Bert has compiled the best leadership axioms in a single book. It's simple, easy-to-read, and well organized. Knowing these principles and putting them into practice will greatly enhance anyone's leadership.

Pastor Dave Engbrecht
Senior Pastor, Nappanee Missionary Church

Good leadership is something we strive for while at the same time gaining experience as a leader. Bert has captured nuggets of truth in leadership helpful in each phase of your journey toward being a good leader. This book helps to point out the importance of learning and demonstrating good leadership skills from the very beginning to the end as you guide your successor and all along your leadership path. This book will be a great reference for you!

Dr. Trish Burgess
Director, Global Health Outreach
Christian Medical & Dental Associations

Outstanding—comprehensive and insightful! There is something for every stage of leadership and more. Not only will you learn more about your own leadership but will get many useful nuggets on how to equip and train future leaders as well. Becoming a better leader is incumbent on the leader to make meaning of their experiences and learn from them. This book takes you on a journey that allows the leader to draw from Bert's vast experience and leadership acumen and apply that which aligns to his core convictions and values.

Tom Hustead, MD
Chief Executive Officer, The Referent Group

In *The Leadership Journal from a Leader's Journey*, you will find a range of leadership insights not found together in any other resource. The gleanings taken from "What I Wish I Knew When I Was New in Leadership" and "Dealing with Criticism" are priceless and worth the price of the book alone, for

I have often seen leaders stumble at these moments, even to the extent they are unable to continue down the path of leadership success. Bert Jones desires to serve leaders on their journey to making life better for those they lead. Allow him to join you on your leadership journey. You and those you lead will be blessed.

Mark Hecht
Founder, Coaching Horizons

Leaders are learners. *The Leadership Journal from a Leader's Journey* is a wonderful collection of leadership insights. Bert Jones opens his leadership journal and shares it with the world so others can glean from the lessons he's learned over his more than three decades of hands-on leadership experience. This book will stir your thinking and challenge you to go deeper and further in your own leadership journey.

Dave McAuley
Founder, Summit Leadership

Whether you are a seasoned leader or just starting the journey, this book is full of practical advice, good reminders, and fundamental principles of leadership. If you have the desire to equip yourself and others to reach their leadership potential, then *The Leadership Journal from a Leader's Journey* provides the framework needed to inspire and impact you and those you influence.

Kevin E. Bish
Vice President of Enrollment Management
and Student Services, Asbury Theological Seminary

The Leadership Journal from a Leader's Journey: Wisdom Learned Along the Way is a treasure trove of insights guaranteed to inspire, encourage, and guide any leader. Bert Jones has put together a wonderful collection of leadership concepts I wish I had known when I started down this path over thirty years ago. Not only will you enjoy this book, but you will find yourself motivated to try new things, and you'll want to give a copy of the book to every leader you know.

Dr. Marcus Warner
Author of *Rare Leadership: 4 Uncommon Habits for Building Trust, Joy, and Engagement in the People You Lead*
(with Dr. Jim Wilder)
President of Deeper Walk International

Dedicated to my first grandchild, Judah Jones, a next-generation leader. May God be praised through your future leadership.

Special thanks to my wife, Cheryl, for her faithful support of my leadership and willingness to travel with me on this journey that has taught me so many life and leadership lessons. Thanks for always being there with me.

The Leadership Journal from a Leader's Journey

Wisdom Learned Along the Way

Bert L. Jones

Christian Medical & Dental Associations was founded in 1931 and currently serves more than 18,000 members. It coordinates a network of Christian healthcare professionals for personal and professional growth; sponsors student ministries in medical and dental schools; conducts overseas healthcare projects for underserved populations; addresses policies on healthcare, medical ethics, and bioethical and human rights issues; distributes educational and inspirational resources; provides missionary healthcare professionals with continuing education resources; and conducts international academic exchange programs.

For more information:
Christian Medical & Dental Associations
P.O. Box 7500
Bristol, TN 37621-7500
888-230-2637
www.cmda.org • main@cmda.org

ISBN: 978-1-7344968-8-8
Library of Congress Control Number: 2022942417
Printed in the United States of America
First Printing: August 2022

Contents

Foreword

If you are like most people, you have at least one prized collection you have patiently and proudly curated over years, maybe even decades, of your life. Throughout grade school and junior high, I built a Lincoln cent and Kennedy half-dollar collection from coins my father gave me as well as coins I discovered in loose change or that my aunts, uncles, and grandparents donated to my cause. Even today, I sometimes pull out my old Whitman coin folders and 1963 *Handbook of United States Coins* and squint at the tiny dates I used to analyze with ease, and without magnification. I am grateful I hung onto these numismatic treasures for four or five decades, through the various travails, transitions, and travels of my life. These coins are extremely valuable to me now, though they don't add any value to my friends or family.

With great care, Pastor Bert Jones has curated a different kind of treasure over a lifetime of studying, observing, and practicing leadership—a collection of truths, teachings, quotes, and notes he discovered "along the way." Bert's fastidious practice of documenting in his own journal about leadership (nearly everything related to leadership he has heard or read, studied or discovered, taught or preached) has resulted in this treasure chest of topical teachings and outlines—a ready-made companion for any serious student or teacher of leadership.

This leadership journal is Bert's third such collection of leadership teachings, with books one and two titled *Leadership Proverbs* and *Servant*

Leadership: Proverbs for Today's Leaders, co-authored with Christian Medical and Dental Associations' CEO Emeritus, Dr. David Stevens.

The old coins I so diligently collected in my youth attained greater value by remaining uncirculated, untouched, and isolated from everyday use. In contrast, the inherent value of the leadership "pearls" in this book come from application, regular practice, frequent demonstration, and repeated testing over time across a broad spectrum of leadership settings by a bevy of practitioners, including Bert Jones himself.

Like a compendium of graduate school topical outlines or detailed class notes, you will not be able to read through this entire resource in just a few hours. You will want to use the notes in this journal, combined with your own leadership experiences, to harvest applications for your own leadership journey. Bert's personal collection of leadership teaching pearls has one more contrast from that precious coin collection of my youth. As I recently looked through my coin folders, I was reminded that I am missing some of the rarest Lincoln cent pieces and Kennedy half-dollars. They were way out of my price range in the 70s and, for the most part, remain that way to this day. As you read and consider Bert's leadership notes and quotes collection, it is likely you will discover deficits in your own leadership practices. I sure did! Don't let that thought dissuade you from reading Bert's journal but inspire you to dig deep in every chapter. Evangelical Christian leader John C. Maxwell, whose quotes appear frequently throughout Bert's journal, said this in his *[The] 21 Irrefutable Laws of Leadership*:

> *"If you and I knew each other personally and we met weekly or monthly to talk about leadership, every time we got together, I'd share with you something new I'd learned. As a person, I continue to grow. I'm constantly reading. I'm analyzing my mistakes. I'm talking to excellent leaders to learn from them. Each time you and I were to sit down, I'd say, 'You won't believe what I just learned.'"*[1]

Though you won't physically be sitting down with Pastor Bert Jones, this leadership journal will help you gain insight into what God taught him as he pastored several churches and led in nonprofit Christian ministries for nearly three decades. I trust your own personal collection of leadership "gold nuggets" will grow in amazing ways as you dive into *The Leadership Journal from a Leader's Journey*.

Dr. Mike Chupp
Chief Executive Officer
Christian Medical & Dental Associations

---

[1] John C. Maxwell, *The 21 Irrefutable Laws of Leadership: Follow Them and People Will Follow You* (Nashville: Thomas Nelson, 1998), Kindle edition Loc 147.

Preface

Leaders never withhold or hoard what is helpful to someone else. They pass along profitable principles to help other people progress in their own journeys. For more than thirty years I have been collecting, connecting, and communicating leadership concepts in my journals. I have written in those journals leadership wisdom, secrets, and lessons I've learned by exploring the scriptures, reading about leadership, interacting with great leaders, and observing my own life experiences.

At the end of each day, I would ask myself two questions: (1) *What did I learn about leadership today?* and (2) *What could someone else have learned about leadership today by following my example?* Through the years, I have learned as many principles from mistakes or bad examples as I have from good ones. Daily, I disciplined myself to write down observations I discovered in that moment. These two questions formed the basis for the previous books I co-authored with Dr. David Stevens, *Leadership Proverbs* and *Servant Leadership*. (Both titles are available through Christian Medical & Dental Associations.)

The book you hold in your hands is not something you read from cover to cover in one sitting. It is a resource gathered from my leadership notebooks over the years that you will hopefully return to again and again to find insight for your own leadership journey. I pray it will be a reference for you as you have opportunities to teach and train leaders in your sphere of influence. This book is a journal of principles, quotes, notes, and insights the Lord has revealed to me as I have tried to grow and develop as a leader through the years. You can distinguish the difference between original content and that which originated from someone else's pen by quotation marks and the name that accompanies the reference. All other content in this journal are lessons from my journey.

Thanks to Dr. Steve Sartori, who served as content editor for this project, and to Terry Bailey, who served as editor and designer. Thanks also to Barbara Snapp for overseeing this project. I appreciate all the work Steve, Terry, and Barbara invested to help me complete this book. I am also grateful for the entire CMDA staff, who has played a part in preparing and producing this leadership resource. Thank you, everyone!

I learned years ago that leaders are readers and continual learners. When you stop yearning for learning, you may as well stop leading. Leadership is the capacity to develop someone or something to reach its fullest potential. I hope the leadership lessons from my leadership journey will inspire you to grow in your understanding and capacity as a leader as well as help you equip and mentor the next generation of future leaders.

Lord Bless,

Bert Jones
Director of Leadership and Church Relations
Christian Medical & Dental Associations

My Leadership Journal

What I Wish I Had Known When I Was New in Leadership

The works of leadership far outweigh the perks of leadership. A lot of people want the title but not the trouble that goes along with the position of leadership.

You may have a position of leadership, but that does not automatically give you permission to proceed with change. You must earn the right to make single and significant change.

To grow an organization to its optimal potential, it is essential for you to first increase your own level of leadership.

Develop organizational systems and standards that will work in almost any leadership setting. Taking time at the beginning of your career to set leadership values and habits will be well worth the investment of time and energy.

Evaluate everything you do. No matter what it is, evaluate it and see how you can improve it. Keep good records so you can review it and revise it next time.

Sometimes the people you trust most will respond to you with something that feels unjust. The people closest to you have the potential to cause you the greatest disappointment and pain.

You cannot force people to go farther than they are willing to go. You can invite followers to join you in your pursuit of excellence, but you cannot insist they come along.

The outcomes of leadership hinge on the amount of time you spend in prayer and the hours you are willing to prepare in advance. Praying and preparing are strategically connected.

On my own, I can do something important. With the help of a team, I can make a greater impact. With a team and the influence and power of the Holy Spirit, I can make an eternal difference.

Don't try to please everybody. You can't make everyone happy.

The Art of a Smart Start

True or False: "It's not how you start but how you finish that counts?" The answer to that question is actually, "Tralse." It is both true and false. It does matter how you finish, but it matters just as much how you start. In leadership and in life, how you start plays an important role in how you finish. Your start is the initial indicator of your probability of success.

5 Types of Starts:

1. The False Start
   - In track and field, a false start results in being disqualified.
   - In football, a false start results in a penalty or loss of yardage.

2. The Failed Start
   - They get ready, get set, but never go.
   - Mark Twain said, "The secret to getting ahead is getting started."

3. The Slow Start
   - You can recover from this position, but you must discover some inner strength and strategy to pull it out. You need a different

frame of mind when you find yourself behind because of a slow start. Put your nose to the grindstone. You've got to get serious to be victorious.

4. The Quick Start
   - This runner starts out strong but doesn't stay there long. Initially he looks great, but because he is not pacing himself, he falls behind.
   - While it looks good at first, it fails in the end.

5. The Smart Start
   - All runners start with a goal in mind. Focus your attention on a few new initiatives. Keep an ongoing list to assist your future plans.
   - An on-ramp is a better way to enter a highway. One of the challenges of starting well is that we often operate from a cold start. Ramp up with an on-ramp.
   - Celebrate your victories. Take a victory lap to celebrate what's been accomplished.

"You don't have to be great to start, but you do have to start to be great." —Zig Zigler

"Take it to the Bank" Leadership Lessons

When my children were growing up and teachable moments arose, I would offer fatherly advice. Often I would conclude with, "And you can take that to the bank." The expression describes something you can know for sure. I began to think of some "take it to the bank" statements regarding leadership. Having been on a three decades long leadership journey, here are some things of which I am certain:

Your character will ultimately characterize your leadership. When your character is not viewed as credible, your leadership will be severely discredited.

Stay humble so you do not stumble. Pride goes before a fall. Humility will enhance your ability to lead others. (Proverbs 16:18)

A strong reputation is developed through the duration of time but can be quickly destroyed when you yield to temptation.

Leaders must always set an example of their expectations.

Leaders need to make allowance for balance in their lives. If they don't, burnout will be the turnout.

Your temperament sets the temperature in your organization.

You will have regular appointments with disappointment in your leadership career. Disappointment, difficulty, and discouragement are inevitable when you are in leadership.

Serving in a leadership role places you in subjection to potential rejection.

It is always wise to seek advice before you take a chance and advance.

Common sense can be your best defense against disaster.

Jealousy in leadership leaves a terrible legacy.

Leaders can be very smart and still have low social intelligence.

Leaders can create credibility or liability through their actions.

Your future is factored by faithfulness.

You can't achieve what you don't believe. Believe all things are possible.

You connect better with people when you honor them and give them respect. People reject those who disrespect them.

You are the one who determines if you will be deterred by discouragement or "beat" by defeat.

Your beliefs influence your behavior.

You will never lead people beyond what you have become. It's the law of the lid.

When you mistreat your team, you create mistrust within your team.

When listening is high on your leadership list, people will be quicker to enlist, support, and serve.

It's hard for things to work out when you're not willing to work hard.

You become an extravagant leader by always giving and going the extra mile. (Matthew 5:41)

A leader's words can wound or ground someone for a lifetime.

You must be ready for what is ahead. The wise are never unprepared for an unprecedented surprise.

Rejection, rather than reflection, of godly correction is foolish decision. (Proverbs 1:25, 30)

A leader needs to remain optimistic regardless of the opposition or projected outlook.

Leaders refuse to be limited by their limitations. Leaders look for a way to go through the obstacle when others are through trying.

A winning leader knows how to press on when the pressure's on.

Little choices can have large consequences.

The context should influence the content.

Every challenge is an invitation for innovation.

The more you prepare in advance, the less there is to repair afterward. Preparation is the best predictor of success.

Determination is the potential differential.

Intention without implementation will never get you to your destination.

You will never accomplish anything you don't attempt.

There is no easy way to get through hardship.

Continuous improvement is the key to advancement.

To attain your goals, you must sustain your growth over a long period of time.

There are no shortcuts to longevity in leadership.

Credibility in leadership is often the outcome of stability in leadership.

To dismiss something without due diligence is pure negligence.

When leaders convey appreciation, their followers will display admiration.

Sometimes nothing said can say it all.

When there are good processes in place, you will be on pace for progress.

Truth prevails in the details.

Cultivating a Leadership Culture

3 Necessary Ingredients for Any Group to be Successful:

1. The influence of a strong leader.
2. The synergy of a gifted and diverse leadership team.
3. The structure that supports an effective and efficient leadership culture.

As a younger leader, I thought my main responsibility was to cultivate my own leadership, but now I see that my main responsibility is to create and cultivate a leadership culture.

When you fail to establish a successful leadership environment, the culture will be strong only if the leader sticks around.

A positive result of establishing a leadership culture is that no one must be the leadership police; policies will be policed by your people.

To cultivate a leadership culture, a leader must:

I. Thoroughly examine the existing leadership culture.
    A. Investigate the history and current culture. When you don't understand your history, you undermine your future.
    B. Interview team members within the current culture. Include insiders as well as outsiders. Listen and learn from them.
    C. Immerse yourself in the current culture.

II. Create an atmosphere where there is a strong leadership agenda.
    A. Lay out a clear plan.
    B. Lay out any new procedures (systems and structure).
    C. Lay out any new policies.
    D. Lay out a clear purpose and direction.
    E. Lay out a positive outlook.

III. Earn the right to implement significant change.
    A. Leaders with credibility and stability have a greater ability to accomplish significant and meaningful change.
    B. Establish trust. Your team must arrive at the place where they trust you before your leadership agenda can begin to thrive.

C. Pick up some early wins and create momentum. Start with small strategic successes.

D. Some change can be implemented immediately while other changes must be introduced instinctively (when the time is right).

IV. Begin to break up the bad habits of the current culture.

    A. Deal with the real issues in your organization.

    B. Make a list of everything that needs to be addressed within your organization and then systematically and diplomatically begin to deal with each issue and individual.

V. Spend prime time with your team.

VI. Establish clear leadership expectations.

VII. Set goals for the whole group and with the whole group.

    A. The team must have a part in the goal-setting process for it to be meaningful and successful. ("You must get weigh-in before you get buy-in." —Patrick Lencioni)

    B. Set strategic and specific goals that are:
        1. Multiple
        2. Meaningful

3. Manageable
4. Measurable
C. Report on the progress of those goals.
    1. Information (that everyone needs to know)
    2. Accomplishments (goals accomplished)
    3. Goals (short-term and long-term)

VIII. Educate leaders at every level of the organization.

A. Regardless of your title. Everyone leads within a leadership culture.
B. Lift the leadership lid of everyone in the organization.

IX. Let your people lead. Avoid hesitation in delegation.

X. Evaluate everything you do as a team and organization.

XI. Make a commitment to continual coaching.

A. Coaches do not just coach during practice or pre-season. They keep coaching even with two or three seconds left in the game.
B. Don't be afraid to use a time-out to address anything that is not working on the court.

XII. Commit your culture to God. (Romans 12:1-2)

When you cultivate a leadership culture, 6 things increase among team members:

1. Activity
2. Productivity
3. Adaptivity
4. Longevity
5. Receptivity
6. Creativity

Cultivating a leadership culture requires:

- Time (patience)
- Trust (buy-in)
- Thought (critical thinking)
- Training (teaching leadership)
- Tenacity (Don't quit.)

Insights into Leadership Intuition

Strong leaders are easy to spot because they show:

- Initiative. They don't have to be told to do something; they automatically act in any given situation. They are self-motivated.
- Innovation. They don't have to do things the way they've always done them.
- Inspiration. They know how to inspire and rally the team.
- Intuition. In their hearts they know what to do. Intuition makes you invaluable in leadership.

Intuition is one of the primary indicators of a great leader.

"All great leaders are gifted with intuition. They know, without reasoning or analysis, what they need to know." —Alexis Carrel

John C. Maxwell teaches that there are 3 levels of leadership intuition:

1. Those who naturally understand leadership.
2. Those who can be nurtured to understand leadership.
3. Those who will never understand leadership.

"I regard leadership intuition as the ability of a leader to read what's going on." —John C. Maxwell

Intuition is defined as the ability to sense or know immediately without reasoning. It is an impression that something might be the case.

Dr. Weston H. Agor describes intuition as "...knowing for sure without knowing for certain...." Others will say it's the same as a hunch, a gut feeling, an instinct, or an inner knowing. Warren Bennis calls it his "inner voice."

I believe intuition is insight without information. It's knowing what to do without knowing why.

10 Reasons Why Intuition is Important in Leadership:

1. Leadership is more art than science.
    - Leaders with intuition have a sense of what to do often before they know the reason why.
    - Leadership is not paint-by-numbers. You must be creative on the canvas of circumstances.
    - Leadership is more formation than formula. Most developing leaders are looking for the quick formula for success

rather than the long-term formation of leadership intuition.

- Given enough information, your intuitive sense will be validated.

2. The DNA of every leadership opportunity is distinctly different.

- Some principles may be appropriate, but not all practices will apply to every given situation.
- Intuition is important because leadership opportunities are never identical.
- What worked in a previous experience is no guarantee the same action will prevail in future experiences.
- "What got you here won't get you there." —Marshall Goldsmith

3. Intuition provides a sneak preview into a potential problem or possibility.

- Intuitive leaders deal with problems and possibilities preemptively.
- "Whenever leaders find themselves facing a problem, they automatically measure it and begin solving it using the law of intuition." —John C. Maxwell
- Intuition is what helps a leader perceive a problem before he can see the problem.

- Intuition is what helps a leader foresee an opportunity before it is obvious to everyone else.

4. Intuition is often the determining factor in what to do first or what to do next.
   - "Good instincts usually tell you what to do long before your head has figured it out." —Michael Burke
   - Too many leaders are stuck because they don't know where to start. They are doing nothing because they don't know what to do next. They need to develop their leadership intuition.
   - In football, it's called the audible. Leaders need to be available for the audible.
   - "Intuition is like a head start in a race." —John C. Maxwell

5. Intuition allows a leader the ability to give an initial response rather than having to fully research the matter.

6. Intuition gives understanding to what otherwise may remain unknown.
   - Intuitive leaders have a sixth sense that helps them pick up on things.

- Too many leaders ignore problems because they don't have the insight to explore potential solutions.

7. Intuition inspires insight into the decision-making process.
   - Intuition is your internal instruction manual.
   - Your leadership intuition is enhanced by your
     o Education (formal and informal)
     o Experiences (cumulative)
     o Exposure to the life experiences of great leaders.
   - The longer you lead in your setting, the greater the impact on your intuition.
   - Intuition integrates your education and experience with other leaders' education and experience.

8. Leadership is not always a matter of right and wrong, but better and best.

9. Intuition gives a leader the competitive and comparative advantage.
   - Intuition is what gives a leader an advantage over the average leader.
   - Leaders are always looking for what gives them the competitive edge; intuition works.

10. Leadership often boils down to a "gut feeling" rather than a "good formula."

To increase your intuition (the acquisition of leadership intuition):

- Train your instincts through education, experience, and exposure.
- Tune into your instincts. Leaders must be in tune with their intuition.
- Trust your instincts. It is the difference between success and settling for something much less.
- Track your instincts. Develop data on what will help you develop your intuition.

"The intuitive mind is a sacred gift, and the rational mind is a faithful servant. We have created a society that honors the servant and has forgotten the gift." —Albert Einstein

"A leader or a man of action in a crisis almost always acts subconsciously (or intuitively) and then thinks of the reasons for his action." —Jawaharlal Neh

Leadership Is Critical in Moments of Crisis

Crisis can confront us in varying degrees, but one thing is certain: crisis will come. Crises don't always come at convenient times.

A crisis will either be the collapse of your leadership or the confirmation of your leadership. Generally, leaders either emerge or submerge during a crisis.

"Character is not made in a crisis; it is only exhibited." —Robert Freeman

"Conflict builds character; crisis defines it." —Steven V. Thulon

Tips on Leading Through Crisis:

I.   Prepare in advance for potential and possible crisis.
   A. Advanced planning is one of the best ways to advance your cause during a crisis.
   B. Too many leaders spend their time repairing from a crisis because they didn't spend any time preparing for the crisis.

C. It is irresponsible for a leader to ignore the possibility of pending crisis.

II. Stay calm in the face of crisis.

   A. Leaders must project calm in the face of crisis.
   B. When a leader does not stay calm in a crisis, it sends the wrong message.
   C. The leader's reaction will often be the response of those who are affected.

III. Seek counsel, not consensus, in times of crisis.

   In moments of crisis, we must move quickly from the advisory stage of leadership into the action stage of leadership; otherwise, our crisis can become a calamity.

IV. Carefully and prayerfully choose your next move.

   A. Your next move can escalate the crisis, ease the crisis, or eliminate the crisis.
   B. Don't forget to bring Christ into your crisis. Seek His will, direction, leading, and peace.

V. Continue to assess and adjust your plan of action.

VI.   Communicate from the front.

A.   In times of crisis, a leader must be both visible and verbal. Too often, crisis drives leaders behind closed doors instead of out into the trenches.

B.   "Leaders are those who know what to do next, know why that is important, and know what appropriate resources to bring to bear on the problem at hand. Then, through effective communication, they influence others to follow." —Barry Bowater

C.   An effective leader will actively advise whenever crises arise. A leader must communicate help and hope during these times.

VII.   Keep things in perspective.

A.   Creating the big picture is one of the most critical things a leader must do. Taking all available information and putting it into an historical or contextual perspective sets up the background where events unfold.

B.   A leader needs to be:

1.   Reflective in preparing a perspective.
2.   Objective in providing a perspective.
3.   Selective in promising through a perspective.
4.   Effective in proclaiming a perspective.

VIII. Glean as much wisdom from the crisis as possible.

A. Crisis is often a course that you must repeat as a leader.

B. "Close scrutiny will show that most crisis situations are opportunities to either advance or stay where you are."
—Maxwell Maltz

C. Crisis or adversity can be a time of great learning and growth. A degree from the University of Adversity is hard earned.

D. Times of crisis are times of great opportunity. The Chinese letter for "crisis" combines two characters—the first designating danger; the second, opportunity.

Value-driven Decisions

There are different kinds of decisions:

- Decisions that are made in volume (multiple decisions at once)
- Decisions that are made in a vacuum (emptiness of space)
- Decisions that are based on certain variables
- Decisions that are based on venture (risk or the lack of it)
- Decisions that have been carefully vetted (thoroughly examined)
- Decisions that are based on values (Values can govern and guide.)

"It's not hard to make decisions when you know what your values are." — Roy Disney

10 Steps in the Value-driven Decision Process:

1. Evaluate the decision at hand.

2. Predetermine your list of core values for that decision.

3. Prioritize your values.

   - Most important to least important
   - It is important to list even the trivial values; they may come into play later, and they may be the determining value as you compare a decision.

4. Establish your non-negotiable values. Which ones put an "end to the bend" (you will not bend on)

5. Communicate your values to everyone involved.

6. Carefully consider all your current options.

7. Compare and contrast your options to your values. Measure each decision by the values you have established.

8. Search out the clear conclusion.

9. Validate your values by staying true to them.

10. Celebrate your decision.

    - This process allows you to be more excited about your decision when you match up your predetermined values with the decision you are making.

Integrity Interference

The word "integrity" comes from the same Latin root as "integer" and implies a wholeness of person. Just as we would talk about a whole number, so also we can talk about a whole person who is undivided. A person of integrity is living rightly, not divided, not being a different person in different circumstances. A person of integrity is the same person in private that he or she is in public.

"Integrity is doing what you said you would do, when you said you would do it, and how you said you would do it." —Byrd Baggett

"Integrity is keeping my commitment even if the circumstances when I made the commitment have changed." —David Jeremiah

"Integrity is what you do when no one is watching; it's doing the right thing all the time, even when it may work to your disadvantage." —Tony Dungy

Integrity infractions have become commonplace in our culture. If you diagnose these infractions, you will usually discover interference. Interference is the act or an instance of hindering, obstructing, or impeding.

The flag will be thrown for integrity interference when you begin to believe: (Note: these beliefs are very dangerous.)

1. You are the exception to the expectation.

2. You deserve something you don't.

3. A good reason overrides a wrong decision.
   - "My reason is reasonable."

4. The end justifies the means.
   - Your actions are appropriate if they accomplish your desired end.

5. Rules were made to bend, amend, and suspend.
   - Rules are a guide but not mandatory to abide.

6. It's not wrong if everybody else is doing it.
   - The popular decision is the proper decision.
   - In sports, it's not always the initiator who gets caught.
   - Wrong is wrong even if everyone is doing it. Right is right even if no one is doing it." —unknown
   - "There is never a right time to do the wrong thing, and never a wrong time to do the right thing." —Lou Holtz

7. Compared to the actions of others, your infractions are insignificant. Integrity is not a sliding scale.

8. It's practical to tell a partial truth when you're facing a serious predicament or problem.

9. You can reply with a little white lie and get by. (Acts 5:1-11)

10. A little lapse of judgment is not big deal in the long run.

11. You have a right to do something wrong if there is a strong chance it will accomplish something good.

12. You will never get caught. No one will ever know. (2 Samuel 11)

13. Shading and evading the truth are not unethical.

14. A little compromise can help you capitalize on a large opportunity.
    - A person can start thinking these conditions warrant a little compromise.

15. If it can be explained, it can be excused.

16. Your personal perception and interpretation of the truth is more important than prevailing authority. "The way I interpret that is..."

17. A clever cover-up will never be exposed. (Numbers 32:23)

18. Your accomplishments exempt you from any accountability.

19. Your position gives you special privileges.

20. Your loyalty and longevity to the company allow you extra latitude when it comes to rules and regulations.
    - Your long-term commitment to the company does not give you a license to commit wrongdoing.

21. Your circumstances give you a decent rationale to circumvent the established code of conduct.
    - You can rationalize anything you realize is problematic.
    - "Real integrity stays in place whether the test is adversity or prosperity." —Charles R. Swindoll

22. A momentary indiscretion will not leave a monumental impression.

23. One time is not a crime.
    - This is great deception because it is simply NOT true and because one time is rarely enough. (It always leads to more.)

The problem is that once we begin to believe these, we deceive ourselves and get called for integrity interference.

Just like in football, when you get called for interference, the penalty can cost you yardage and, ultimately, the game.

"Integrity is the glue that holds our way of life together. We must constantly strive to keep our integrity intact. When wealth is lost, nothing is lost; when health is lost, something is lost; when character is lost, all is lost." —Billy Graham

"Be more concerned with your character than your reputation because your character is what you really are, while your reputation is merely what others think you are." —John Wooden

Imitate a leader whose focus is on their integrity, not their image. Image-driven leadership can be very dangerous.

A leader must be careful not to become careless with his character.

1. THE RESUMÉ SEASON (1 Samuel 16:11; 17:15, 33-37)

   In the same way that a resumé is a specific summary of a person's previous employment, experiences, and education, this season is a learning time, a time to gather and to gain experiences.

   "Leadership and learning are indispensable to each other." —John F. Kennedy

   The key to this season of life is to take advantage of life's opportunities.

   You must build your reputation and references in this season.

   You never know how a good reference today will make a difference tomorrow.

   Young leaders often burn bridges in their past instead of building bridges for their future. Your resumé season will always return to haunt you or to help you. All extraordinary leaders have some ordinary experience in their resumé.

2. THE RECOGNITION SEASON (1 Samuel 16:12, 13)

David didn't get mad that he didn't get dressed that day. He was surprised when he got recognized.

If you must tell someone you're a leader, you're not! People who try to be recognized are usually not.

Your actions always attract more attention than attempts to sell yourself.

It is your record, not your rhetoric, in this season that gets you recognized as a leader. It's your work, not your words, that will prove and promote your leadership. The proof is in what you can produce. (Daniel 6:3)

Real leaders are not recognized because they sell themselves but because they are serving someone else. If you are a leader out serving in the field, you will be sought out! The key to this season is to stay out in the field serving. It is where your leadership will be revealed.

Leaders are revealed on the battlefield, not in a beauty pageant. While David's brothers are being paraded in front of Samuel, David shows his stuff on the battlefield.

The best way to serve in a position of leadership is to position yourself in a place of service. When you see a leader at work, you don't have to wonder if they will work out as a leader. Leaders are not chosen because they deserve to be but because they serve to be.

3. THE RESPONSIBILITY SEASON (1 Samuel 16:14-23; 18:5)

This is a season when you are selected to serve for a special task.

Future leaders seem to desire all the rights and privileges of leadership without dealing with the responsibilities that come with those leadership roles.

When it comes to taking responsibility, there are two kinds of leaders: those who want to avoid it and those who are willing to accept it.

"The price of greatness is responsibility."
—Winston Churchill

How far you go in leadership is often determined by how faithful you are in this season. (Matthew 25:23; Luke 19:17)

The key to this season is to commit your best, no matter how big or small the job. People who take small tasks seriously are usually taken seriously as a leader.

4. THE REFINING SEASON (1 Samuel 18:8-2 Samuel 4)

This is a season of testing, training, tempering, teaching, and trusting—of not just going, but growing, through challenges. This season often comes on the heels of success.

Leaders often emerge during an emergency. It can be a refining time for leaders. Whining doesn't do you a lot of good in the refining season.

The key to this season is to complete the course and not quit. There is no credit for an incomplete course. People who drop out before the course is over usually drop behind in being prepared to lead. They give out, give in, and give up before they get a chance to grow up and go up.

5. THE REIGNING SEASON (2 Samuel 5)

This season is when you have been given the authority to make decisions in leadership. You are in charge.

Power either goes to your head or to your hand. If it goes to your head, it leads to pride; if it goes to your hand, you put your hand to action. The key in the reigning season is to remain true to what got you there. These leaders stay the same when they begin to reign. Too many leaders play the fool when they get a chance to rule. Power can poison a person.

"Nearly all men can stand adversity, but if you want to test a man's character, give him power." —Abraham Lincoln

"Power tends to corrupt, and absolute power corrupts absolutely." —Lord Acton

Leaders never stop learning, even at this level of leadership.

Recruiting a team at this stage will depend on how successful you were in the previous seasons. Successful leaders secure dynamic teams. They usually come from people they have met through the seasons of their leadership.

6. THE REPLACEMENT SEASON (1 Kings 1:28; 1 Kings 2)

A great leader will set up their successor for success. A smart leader will not wait until the end to spend time looking for a replacement.

"Success without a successor is failure."
—John C. Maxwell

7. THE REMEMBERED SEASON (Acts 13:22, 36)

While the story of David is an Old Testament story, they are still talking about him in the New Testament.

One of the signs of a remarkable leader is not just the mark they leave on history, but how they are remembered throughout history.

One of the reasons so few leaders are remembered well is that they failed to finish well. The service you render as a leader will determine how you will be remembered. A true sign that a leader is remembered well is that they are referred to often; they are quoted and noted often.

The end of your leadership does not have to the be the end of your legacy.

There are two keys to this season: how you lived and how you led.

"Men make history, not the other way around. In periods where there is no leadership, society stands still. Progress occurs when courageous, skillful leaders seize the opportunity to change things for the better." —Harry S. Truman

More on The Seasons of Leadership:

Too many leaders are interested in the position of leadership, the prestige of leadership, and the power of leadership without going through the process of leadership.

"It is a mistake to look too far ahead. The chain of destiny can only be grasped one link at a time." —Winston Churchill

While potential is essential to success, it does not always guarantee it. Your potential has the power to be instrumental or detrimental in your leadership journey.

You cannot be a seasoned leader without going through the seasons of leadership.

The Leadership Bill of Rights

I. A leader must live right. When we talk about leadership, we talk about what leaders do. Before Paul addressed with Timothy what leaders do, he addressed what leaders need to be. (1 Timothy 3:2, 8) One of the first responsibilities of leadership is to live right.

   A. A leader must maintain a right attitude. A negative attitude will negate a positive influence. Your attitude will affect your altitude as a leader.

   B. "The last of the human freedoms—to choose one's attitude in any given set of circumstances." —Viktor Frankl

   C. "Attitude is a little thing that makes a big difference." —Winston Churchill

   D. "Ability is what you're capable of doing. Motivation determines what you do. Attitude determines how well you do it." —Lou Holtz

II. A leader must always do what is right. (Micah 6:8; Genesis 4:7; Exodus 15:26; Deuteronomy 6:18)

III. A leader must do the right things.

    A. Even beyond doing what is right, a leader must do the right things.

    B. One of the toughest skills in leadership is making decisions about what to do and what not to do.

    C. "Management is doing things right; leadership is doing the right things." —Peter Drucker

    D. "Management is efficiency in climbing the ladder of success; leadership determines whether the ladder is leaning against the right wall." —Stephen R. Covey

IV. A leader must do things right from the start. If it's worth doing, it's worth doing right. If it's worth doing right, it's worth doing right from the beginning.

V. A leader must be willing to deal with situations right away. Deal quickly and delicately. Things don't go away unless you deal with them right away. Things don't go away just because you delay dealing with them.

VI. A leader must earn the right to make changes.

VII. A leader should not veer to the right or the left of his vision and mission.

> A leader must know who he is, what he is, and how he is going to accomplish his mission and vision. He cannot afford to allow people to hijack his mission and vision.

VIII. A leader must be willing to ask the right kinds of questions.

> Those questions will often be tough questions to ask. Sometimes leadership is more about asking the right questions than giving the right answers.

IX. A leader must get the right people on his team.

> "Get the right people on the bus, the wrong people off the bus, and the right people in the right seats." —Jim Collins

X. A leader must make things right that are wrong or that have been mishandled. (1 Samuel 12:3)

> Sometimes a correction is the best way to get moving in the right direction. Sometimes you need to go backward to go forward.

XI. A leader must get the timing right on any decision.

John C. Maxwell provides a good formula to remember regarding timing and decision making:

- The wrong decision at the wrong time equals disaster.
- The wrong decision at the right time equals a mistake.
- The right decision at the wrong time equals unacceptable.
- The right decision at the right time equals success.

XII. A leader must be willing to sacrifice his personal rights for the greater good of the people he serves.

7 Fundamentals of Leadership

1. Character and integrity help you to know who you are. They are the cornerstone of leadership longevity.

    Get a handle on potential scandals:
    *   "Your competency will take you only as far as your character will sustain you." —Carey Nieuwhof
    *   Leadership is much less about what you do, and much more about who you are. If you view leadership as a bag of manipulative tricks or charismatic behaviors to advance your own personal interests, then people have every right to be cynical. But if your leadership flows, first and foremost, from inner character and integrity of ambition, then you can justly ask people to lend themselves to your organization and its mission." —Jim Collins

    Establish your essential beliefs early then execute them every time your character is challenged in both little and big things.

2. Observation and evaluation help you to know where you are.

One of your first job assignments as a leader is assessment.

"The first responsibility of a leader is to define reality." —Max De Pree

3 Levels of Observation:
- Blind observation (does not see anything, Matthew 15:14)
- Biased observation (sees things from one point of view)
- Balanced observation (looks at things objectively)

The reverse Golden Rule: Evaluate yourself like you would evaluate someone else who had just done the same thing.

3. Vision and dreams help you to know where you want to be.

"Vision is a clear mental image of a preferable future, imparted by God to His chosen servants and is based upon an accurate understanding of God, self, and circumstances." —George Barna

"Vision is foresight with insight, based on hindsight." —unknown

4. Intuition and strategy help you to know how to get where you want to be.

   Once a leader knows two key points—where he is and where he wants to be—he begins to chart out a course. A leader must be intentional about developing intuition skills.

5. Determination and hard work help you to know the cost of getting where you want to be.

   A lack of determination can be a real detriment to your leadership.

   "The three great essentials to achieve anything worthwhile are first, hard work; second, stick-to-itiveness; third, common sense." —Thomas Edison

   "The price of success is hard work, dedication to the job at hand, and the determination that whether we win or lose, we have applied the best of ourselves to the task at hand." —Vince Lombardi

   Someone once said, "Leadership works if the leader works."

6. Teamwork and networks help you to know who it will take on your team to get you to your destination.

   Vince Lombardi said, "Individual commitment to a group effort—that is what makes a team work, a company work, a society work, a civilization work."

   "Teamwork is the ability to work together toward a common vision. The ability to direct individual accomplishment toward organizational objectives. It is the fuel that allows common people to attain uncommon results." —Andrew Carnegie

   "Leadership is having a compelling vision, a comprehensive plan, relentless implementation, and talented people working together." —Alan Mulally

7. Trust and confidence help other people to know it's safe to follow you.

   You are not leading until you reach this point. Trust is the thrust of leadership, and it takes time. Over time, a leader either develops or destroys the trust of the people on their team. Confidence is not a coincidence! It is established through experiences.

Larry Bird once said, "First master the fundamentals."

Being faithful to fundamentals is instrumental to long-term success. Anytime you view fundamentals as incidental, it can be detrimental to your game.

More on Fundamentals of Leadership:

The great football coach Vince Lombardi began every new season with a lecture to both veterans and rookies on the basics of football. He held up a football and said, "This is a football. Execute the fundamentals, and the rest will follow."

We tend to focus on techniques and tactics instead of basics. We get sidetracked by incidentals instead of getting strong by focusing on fundamentals.

"Success is neither magical nor mysterious. Success is the natural consequence of consistently applying the basic fundamentals." —Jim Rohn

8 Things to Remember When God Places a Vision in Your Heart (Acts 7:20-36. Key verse, vs. 23)

We often give more attention to a vision statement than to the state of the vision. Vision comes from the heart, not from a hard copy (a piece of paper).

1. Your vision can be impaired by your own insight. (vs. 22)
   - Moses was learned in all the wisdom of the Egyptians and was mighty in words and deeds.
   - In other words, that should have fully prepared him to be successful.
   - But God's ways our not our ways. His ways are higher than our ways. (Isaiah 55:8-9)
   - God had to get the "Egypt" out of Moses before He could use Moses to get the people out of Egypt.
   - Hudson Taylor said, "God's work done in God's way will never lack God's supply." The reverse is also true: God's work done in the world's way is worthless.

     BHAG (Big Hairy Audacious Goal) should mean "Big Hand of Almighty God."

2. Your vision can be the right thing but at the wrong time. (vs. 24a)
   - When it comes to successful vision, timing is everything.

3. Your vision can be fully appropriate but not fully appreciated. (vs. 24)
   - Too many leaders have abandoned their God-given vision because they did not get the appreciation they expected.
   - Remember, your vision is to please the Lord, not men. (Galatians 1:10)
   - "...for they loved the praise of men more than the praise of God." (John 12:43)

4. Your vision can be clear in your own mind and still be unclear to others. (vs. 25)
   - You can see it so clearly and it be "clear as mud" to someone else.
   - He supposed (assumed) they understood.
   - The vision may not be clear the first time they hear.
   - "The future belongs to those who see possibilities before they become obvious."
     —John Scully

5. Your vision can be a burden in your heart and still not have buy-in from others. (vs. 27)
   - Because you believe it does not mean they will automatically believe it.
   - A leader can be passionate about his vision and his followers be passive about his pursuits.

- "There is no more powerful an engine driving an organization toward excellence and long-range success than an attractive, worthwhile, achievable vision for the future widely shared." —Burt Nanus, Visionary Leadership
- You will discover that although vision is a preferred picture of the future, not everyone is looking through the same lens.
- Would you rather share an inspired vision or inspire a shared vision?

6. Your vision can meet a critical need and still be criticized. (vs. 27-28)
   - A lot of people are blindsided because they believed they would not be criticized if they fulfilled their calling.

7. Your vision can be put off but not put away. (vs. 29)
   - Moses fled instead of led. If it is a vision from God, it will not go away. It can be delayed, but it will not disappear. God may put it on layaway, but it will not go away.
   - One of the ways to know if you have a God-sized vision is whether it goes away.

8. Your vision can be selected by God and still be rejected by men. (vs. 35)

Before You Venture into Your Vision

Give your vision back to God. A surrendered vision is a more successful vision.

Give your vision time to mature.

Give your vision time to simmer on the stove of your heart.

Give your vision a chance to capture hearts.
- Make it compelling.
- Make it concrete.
- Make it concise.
- Make it contagious.

Give your vision power through preparation.
- Preparation and perspiration produce great results.

Give your vision credibility through confirmation.
- Remember Gamaliel's advice: "If it's of the Lord, you can't stop it or deny it" (Acts 5:33-42).
- When you give your vision time to mature, it becomes clearer in your own mind. As you wait, God will confirm. Once it is clear in your mind and confirmed, you will share it more convincingly and with more conviction.

Cast your vision with confidence.
- "The very essence of leadership is [that] you have a vision. It's got to be a vision you articulate clearly and forcefully on every occasion. You can't blow an uncertain trumpet." —Theodore Hesburgh

Let your vision attract attention through your actions.
- Actions really do speak louder than words. Doing and dreaming must go hand in hand.
- "Vision without execution is hallucination." —Thomas Edison

Vision without action is a daydream. Action without vision is a nightmare." —Japanese proverb

"All successful people—men and women—are big dreamers. They imagine what their future could be, ideal in every respect, and then they work every day toward their distant vision, that goal or purpose." —Brian Tracy

"The vision must be followed by the venture. It is not enough to stare up the steps; we must step up the stairs." —Vance Havner

"Leadership is the capacity to translate vision into reality." —Warren Bennis

"Leaders establish the vision for the future and set the strategy for getting there. They cause change. They motivate and inspire others to go in the right direction. And they, along with everyone else, sacrifice to get there."
—John Kotter

Remember this about vision:
The vision must be REVIEWED from time to time.
The vision must be REVISED from time to time.
The vision must be REPEATED over and over.

"People buy into the leader before they buy into the vision." —John C. Maxwell

"Vision: a mental picture of what could be fueled by a passion that it should be. Vision doesn't stick; it doesn't have natural adhesive; instead, vision leaks." —Andy Stanley

"Vision is a picture of the future that produces passion." —Bill Hybels

"A vision without a task is but a dream. A task without a vision is drudgery. A vision with a task is the hope of the world." —a church in Sussex, England, c. 1730

24 Things Wise Leaders Accomplish Within 24 Hours

This list is not necessarily in order of priority. Often, it is to your advantage to accomplish these things sooner if possible. There may be exceptions to this list. There may be times when it is completely appropriate for you NOT to act within a 24-hour time frame. This list is not exhaustive; there may be other things you deem necessary to accomplish within 24 hours. You may develop a longer list than 24 in your leadership. It is not advisable to attack this list all at once. Slowly implement these practices into your leadership performance, and it will give you a leadership edge. It is the combination of the items on this list that yields a cumulative effect.

1. Return all phone calls, emails, texts, and messages.

2. Take initial action on a decision. Put an action plan in place.

3. Acknowledge the initial receipt of a gift or act of kindness and say thank you. Show appropriate appreciation.

4. Be intentional about recognition and encouragement for a job well done (the power of positive reinforcement through recognition).

5. Open, read, and respond to all mail.

6. Document and organize any new, creative, and innovative ideas or information.

7. Give credit where credit is due. Pass on the praise to others!

8. Update your To-Do list. Better yet, put as many things as you can on your calendar instead of on your To-Do list, along with allocated times for completing them.

9. Assume responsibility for any actions, reactions, factions, transactions, inactions, or infractions that ultimately come under your authority before they become distractions.

10. Research a matter fully before making a final decision.

11. Follow up and follow through on what you say you'll do.

12. Deal with a delayed deadline. Create and communicate NEW details to everyone involved.

13. Be willing to address a mess. Tackle your tough troubles; don't put them off.

14. "If it's your job to eat a frog, it's best to do it first thing in the morning. And if it's your job to eat two frogs, it's best to eat the biggest one first." —Mark Twain

15. Show compassion to someone in a crisis. Lend a helping hand to someone in need. When you delay acting on a need, you delay the blessing that will come when you meet that need.

16. Review and respond to all requests. Develop a method of organization that will help you answer all requests in a timely and effective manner.

17. Report on responsibilities and tasks that have been delegated to you by someone else.

18. Publicize new information and decisions.

19. Notify someone on your team about something you noticed that could either be improved or removed. Feedback is a great way to help someone move forward.

20. Deal with an anger issue. Make sure you calm down before you confront.

21. Contact someone who keeps coming to your mind. You can really impact someone when you act on an impression.

22. Say "I'm sorry" for anything that was said or done in an insensitive or inappropriate manner. Settle offenses quickly.

23. Make final preparation for a presentation. The last 24 hours before a presentation are critical.

24. Make right anything that has been done wrong. Connect and correct.

25. (BONUS) Thank God every day for His blessings and benefits.

More on Accomplishing Things:
- The 4 Ds for discerning task management: Do, Delete, Delegate, Defer.
- The OHIO principle: Only Handle It Once.

Making Adjustments in Leadership

One of the important rules of leadership is you must be able to adjust. You must adjust and adapt to the current challenge.

Great leaders do the following well:

1. Develop a system that will increase the team's potential for success: "Here is what we do and how we do it."

    - The system will not guarantee success, but it will strengthen the prospect for success.
    - Engage the team in creating the system. Weigh-in promotes buy-in.

2. Create a culture where excellence is expected.

3. Vigorously train and equip team members on the expectations for excellence.

4. Relentlessly plan, prioritize, and prepare for the future. Keep the immediate and long term in mind. Focus on the NOW and the WHAT'S NEXT.

5. Courageously adjust along the way. Course correct, adapt, and adjust.

- "Failure isn't fatal, but failure to change might be." —John Wooden
- "Not everything that is faced can be changed, but nothing can be changed until it is faced." —James Baldwin

6. Never give up. Never quit.
   - "Never give in—never, never, never, never, in nothing great or small, large, or petty, never give in except to convictions of honor and good sense. Never yield to force; never yield to the apparently overwhelming might of the enemy." —Winston Churchill
   - "Success is the ability to go from one failure to another with no loss of enthusiasm." —Winston Churchill

Leadership Advice on Adjusting:

1. Give your plan enough time to produce.
   - Don't adjust too quickly. Sometimes you must play out your plan.

2. Don't wait until it's too late to make a necessary change.
   - When you refuse to adjust, you must live with the results.

3. Shuffle your regular routine whenever possible to learn to trust your ability to adjust.
   - People who don't change up their regular routine can't be ready for change. Practice switching up something that is insignificant, and you will have greater confidence switching up something that is significant. Stay flexible.

4. "The easier it is to do, the harder it is to change." —Eng's Principle

5. You must be objective to be corrective.
   - If you lose objectivity, you lose. Don't let your feelings negatively impact your dealings. Be careful not to allow your emotions to cloud your judgment.

6. Measure and manage the magnitude of the tweak.
   - Sometimes you must make a minute adjustment. Sometimes you must make a major adjustment.

7. Understand that criticism will generally accompany an adjustment.
   - People don't generally like change, even if it is a good change.

8. Regularly refine and align your adjustments to fit your current challenge.
   - Stop making excuses and start adjusting.
   - Leaders with the ability to adapt and adjust will have an advantage over those who don't. They will be the ones holding the trophy at the end of the game.
   - Resilience is the ability to adapt to change and recover from adversity, an important leadership trait.

Pioneer	Re-engineer
Starting from scratch	Scratching your head
Spontaneous	Conscientious
No boundaries (free)	Known boundaries (fences)
Inventing	Inventorying
Value excellence	Value existence
Untraditional approach	Traditional approach
Content is everything	Context is everything
Acceleration	Assessment
Defining	Redefining
Work with who you can get	Work with who you have
Creative thinking	Confined thinking
Resources are scarce	Resources are stingy
Create momentum	Create monuments
Fascination with the future	Fascination with the past
Have vision but short on stuff	Have stuff but short on vision
Sense of expectancy	Sense of expectations
Ambitious	Cautious
Spirit of inspiration prevails	Spirit of reservation prevails
Open to change	Opposition to change

Here is what I've noticed about change in a
re-engineering context:

Change happens over time, not overnight.

- This is a significant mindset if you want to
  move change forward.
- Not understanding this simple truth will
  ultimately undermine your prospects for
  change.

- A visionary leader in this setting will look far ahead and see what needs to be done and then map out a course of change that will take place over time.
- Good leaders make changes at a tolerable rate.

Change cannot be rushed.
- A leader can point it in the right direction, but if it is perceived that he is being pushy, he can cause change paralysis.
- You can lead the process of change, but you cannot always speed the process of change.
- Change cannot be rushed, even when you know what is right and what needs to be done, or if you know that if you did it immediately, it would bring instantaneous results.
- GO SLOW and make sure everyone is in the KNOW.
- Change must be graciously introduced and gradually implemented.
- When you rush change, you can ruin the results.
- This whole process can be very frustrating for a visionary leader. Because change can be very slow, leaders can mistakenly perceive that there is no progress being made.

Change must be prioritized.
- You build momentum with change that works. Change must be prioritized and optimized.

Change cannot be left to chance.

- You must arrange your change. Change should be calculated.

Change requires a champion.

- The right kind of change does not happen automatically. There must be someone in charge of a change.

You cannot charge ahead with change unless you change the thinking of those involved. It's called stinking thinking.

- You must change a mindset before managing change. It takes training, teaching, and talking.
- "Progress is impossible without change, and those who cannot change their minds cannot change anything." —George Bernard Shaw

Change will either move you forward in your vision or toward division.

- That will all depend on your diplomacy of implementation.
- A leader must keep the pulse of the people in the process of change. Intuition is important.

You must give change a chance to work. Change takes time.

- It's the difference between turning a jet ski and a battleship.
- After the implementation of a change, it can take some time for people to get used to something new.
- 4 key factors in how long change takes:
  - By-laws that govern the organization
  - Size of the group trying to change
  - Age of the organization
  - Support from the group being changed

Change can often be met with greater resistance than acceptance.

- Especially when we've been doing it this way for a long time.
- Or when we think what we're doing is still working.
- "Any change, even change for the better, is always accompanied by drawbacks and discomforts." —Arnold Bennett
- People tend to resist and reverse change. People try to go back to Egypt when the Promised Land is in sight. (Numbers 14:4)
- Change imposed is change opposed.

Resistance to change is usually more for senti-
mental reasons than substantial reasons.
- People don't have to have a good reason to
  resist change.

Change can be costly.
- Don't pursue change without considering the
  cost. (Luke 14:28)
- Change can often result in casualties.

Change can be subtle and still be substantial.
- Incremental change can still be incredible.
  A minor change can have major impact.

Change is not climaxed at the moment of decision
making. Look at the process of change:
- The appeal for change (situation)
- The approach to change (orientation)
- The approval for change (decision)
- The application of change (implementation)
- The appraisal of change (evaluation)
- The applause of change (celebration)

Change must be presented in a way that people do
  not feel pressured or threatened.

Change must be more sold than told. Don't
  announce a change without introducing change.

Some change is not worth it in the end.
- Weigh the battle with the benefit. The finished product may not be worth the fight. Choose your battles wisely.

Have a good reason for the season of change you are leading.
- Don't just change for the sake of change. Let vision drive your decisions.

Change is rarely comfortable and almost never easy.
- Change can be very frustrating and fulfilling at the same time.

Change demands buy-in from more than just the leader. Your people must embrace change before they can embark on change.

A good reason to change does not automatically give you the right to make a change.

You can have authority to make a change and still need authorization to make the change.

Effective change requires proper education and preparation.
- Preparation and education are key to effective implementation.

- "People will change either when they hurt enough that they have to, or they have learned enough that they want to, or received enough that they are able to."
—John C. Maxwell

Change requires longer commitment and more patience because it is more complicated.

Change requires compromise on all sides involved. Think "win-win" for everyone.

Constant change can create great animosity. Continual change can be counterproductive.

Change can take its toll on those in charge.

Change that is irrelevant is irresponsible. Be careful with careless change. Don't change for change's sake.

Change must be more strategic than spontaneous.

A change agent must understand the agenda of change.
- If you have the responsibility of bringing change in a re-engineering setting, that may be the only role you play.

- It's funny, but a lot of change can happen, and you would think people would be GLAD, but often they're just MAD at the person who upset the fruit basket.
- If you are a change agent, you must understand your role in the agenda of significant change.
- People may be more apprehensive about you than appreciative of you when you are leading change.

More on the Challenges of Change:

Change requires "change" in your pocket. (a John C. Maxwell principle)

Change that works requires a lot of work.

Document the changes you are implementing.

Be careful about changing for the sake of change. A leader must put as much energy into selling the change as he does setting the change. Be cautious about implementing change immediately.

You will never implement a change that makes everyone completely happy.

The longer something has been in place, the longer it takes to make the change.

It is always a good idea to investigate the possible change before you implement it. Determine what the sacred cows are.

A good leader will get buy-in before he brings about significant change.

Don't leave change to chance. Prepare for it. Lead through it. Then you can celebrate its success. Arrange your change.

The Leader as Decision Maker

Decision making is hard when everyone is looking on.

- "Be willing to make decisions. That's the most important quality in a good leader. Don't fall victim to what I call the 'ready-aim-aim-aim-aim syndrome.' You must be willing to fire."
  — George S. Patton

One observation about all great leaders, they are outrageously courageous in their decision-making ability.

- "It takes courage not only to make decisions, but to live with those decisions afterward."
  —Coach K
- "Not having the chance to make decisions within the organization in which one works is a great tragedy, leading to hopelessness and despair." —Max De Pree

10 Decision Making Principles:

1. The person closest to the situation should make the decision.
   - "I call this the proximity principle. The principle of subsidiarity (Catholic social principle): nothing should be done by a larger and more complex organization that

can be done as well by a smaller and simpler organization." —Steve Sartori

That presupposes 4 things:

- o You have the right person in the right position.
- o You have taught the right person the right process to make the right decision.
- o You have the right mechanism and markers in place to monitor and manage the decision.
- o You have the right means for measuring the success of the decision.
- "Empowering means defining the parameters in which people are allowed to operate and then setting them free." —Captain D. Michael Abrashoff

2. Set decision deadlines. Without deadlines, your decisions will continue to be delayed.

3. Let the vision drive the decision. The vision of the organization ought to affect every decision made in the organization.

4. Analyze before you finalize.
   - Gather as much information as possible.
   - Gather the most up-to-date information as possible.

- Gather the wisest advisers possible.
- Gather as many opinions as possible. Wise leaders will look at adverse and diverse opinions.
- Gather as many options as possible. Check your options before you select your outcome.

5. As a decision maker, respect the people who the decision will affect.
   - A caring leader will reflect and respect how the decision will affect others on the team or in the organization. Realize that when you make a decision, it affects more than just you.

6. A great leader understands the priming of timing. When it comes to decision making, timing is everything.

7. As a rule, don't raid a decision once it has been made. It will be overbearing to your decision-making team if you are always overturning their decisions once they are made. People generally complain when you don't refrain from reversing decisions.

   ONE EXCEPTION: Don't go long if you've made the wrong decision.

8. Be slow to make a decision when you're feeling low.
   - Tired
   - Discouraged
   - Defeated
   - Depressed
   - Frustrated
   - Angry
   - Burned out
   - Under pressure

   "...the H.A.L.T. method. Never make a decision when you are Hungry, Angry, Lonely, or Tired." —David DeNotaris

9. If you're not sold on a decision, put the decision on hold (24-hour waiting period). An answer to your decision will often begin to glimmer once you let it simmer.

10. The ABCs of AFTER a decision is made:

    A—Accept it, even if it goes against how you voted.
    - "When we are debating an issue, loyalty means giving me your honest opinion, whether you think I'll like it or not. Disagreement at this stage stimulates me. But once a decision has been made, the debate ends. From that point on, loyalty

means executing the decision as if it were your own." —Colin Powell

- Great decision makers choose what is right regardless of who was right.

B—Back it.

C—Communicate it properly.

D—Delegate it. Making the decision is only part of the process. Once a decision has been made, you must delegate tasks so the new decision can be implemented properly.

- "No decision has been made unless carrying it out in specific steps has become someone's work assignment and responsibility." —Peter F. Drucker

E—Evaluate it. At some point after the decision has been made, you must go back and measure how it is working.

- "It is not always what we know or [have] analyzed before we make a decision that makes it a great decision. It is what we do after we make the decision to implement and execute it that makes it a good decision." —William Pollard

Learn from your mistakes.

- "Most discussions of decision making assume that only senior executives make decisions or that only senior executives' decisions matter. This is a dangerous mistake." —Peter Drucker

More on The Leader as Decision Maker:

Never assume an insignificant decision made today will not have a significant impact tomorrow.

Never assume the information you already know is enough to make the best decision. As a leader, get into the practice of verifying before you make a verdict.

Never assume your team will buy in to a decision if they did not have a chance to weigh in on the decision.

Never assume that because you are being criticized for a decision, a correction must be made. Sometimes your loudest critics will attack you when you've made the right decision and are going in the right direction.

Never assume that because you made the right decision, there will not be repercussions with that decision. It is impossible to please everyone. Good decisions can potentially have bad consequences.

- "You can please some of the people all of the time, you can please all of the people some of the time, but you can't please all of the people all of the time." —John Lydgate

Never assume that because the decision you made today was the right one, it will be the right one tomorrow. Different circumstances might require different conclusions.

Leadership Requires Listening

"Everyone should be quick to listen..." (James 1:19, NIV)

"He who has ears, let him hear." (Matthew 11:15, 13:9, NIV)

"He who answers before listening, that is his folly and his shame." (Proverbs 18:13, NIV)

People love a leader who listens well. John Wooden said, "Listen if you want to be heard."

8 Reasons Why Leaders Are Naturally Lousy Listeners:

Leaders are by nature:
1. Impatient. It takes time to really listen to someone.
2. Problem solvers. They are immediately trying to solve the problem. They want to fix it, not talk about how they feel about it.
3. Time-Conscious. They can sometimes see listening as a waste of time.
4. Communicators. They are talkers, not listeners. They like to give orders, not take orders.
5. Thinkers. Everything said triggers a reaction and response, and they feel like they will explode if they don't share.

6. Busy. They already have a lot on their plate. Genuine listening is often seen as an interruption.
7. Doers. There is not a lot of action involved in listening.
8. Defensive. Once someone throws something critical at them, they immediately start to defend.

Good listeners are actively listening for:

- Silence that speaks louder than words
- What is said clearly and verbally
- What is not being said but is implied
- What is not verbalized but is being said through body language
- What is being said by tone or inflection
- What is being spoken through someone else
- What is being repeated throughout the conversation

Benefits of Listening:

The leader who listens well will gain:
- Valuable information and knowledge
- Understanding
- Insight
- Perspective
- Compassion

- The support and respect of those who are speaking
- The ability to make good judgments
- Good ground on moving the conversation forward
- Trust

"You learn when you listen. You earn when you listen—not just money, but respect."
—Harvey Mackay

"If you listen longer than most people listen, you'll hear things most people never hear."
—Cary Nieuwhof

"Being heard is so close to being loved that for the average person, they are almost indistinguishable."
—David Augsberger

12 Tips on Listening Carefully:

1. Listen by laying down what you are doing and giving your full attention to the person who is speaking to you.
2. Listen by looking directly into the eyes of the person speaking to you.
3. Listen by taking a few notes on what is being spoken to you.
4. Listen with a humble and teachable spirit.

5. Listen by repeating back to the person what has been reported to you. Make sure your understanding matches their intention.
6. Listen without interrupting or interpreting what is being said before the person speaking is finished.
   - "Most people do not listen with the intent to understand; they listen with the intent to reply. They are either speaking or preparing to speak." —Stephen Covey
7. Listen without being defensive in your demeanor.
8. Listen without feeling you must solve the problem. Sometimes when someone gets a chance to verbalize something, a solution appears.
9. Listen and then ask probing questions that show you were listening. Answers are not always necessary.
10. Listen intently through what is being spoken to gain insight into what is unspoken.
11. Ask yourself, "(WAIT) Why Am I Talking?"
12. LISTEN and SILENT have the same letters.

"Courage is what it takes to stand up and speak; courage is also what it takes to sit down and listen." —Winston Churchill

"I only wish I could find an institute that teaches people how to listen. Businesspeople need to listen at least as much as they need to talk. Too many people fail to realize that real communication goes in both directions."
—Lee Iacocca

"Listening, not imitation, may be the sincerest form of flattery." —Dr Joyce Brothers

"Listening is the single skill that makes the difference between a mediocre and a great company." —Lee Iacocca

"We must be silent before we can listen. We must listen before we can learn. We must learn before we can prepare. We must prepare before we can serve. We must serve before we can lead."
—William Arthur Ward

Leaders listen; followers just wait until it's their turn to talk.

Leaders learn and leverage more because they listen to their people. (2 Samuel 7:1-29)

A Servant Leader

A servant leader is willing to serve others first
without serving their own self-interest.

A servant leader is willing to tackle any size task
without complaining. (Philippians 2:14)

A servant leader is willing to provide leadership
without wearing a prominent title. A title does
not entitle you to lead. In fact, a title does not
prove anything in leadership. Service, not status,
is what makes a great leader.

A servant leader is willing to remain teachable
without reacting in offense.

A Servant leader is willing to receive criticism
without comprising a comeback. (Matthew
27:14)

A servant leader is willing to work hard without
recognition or reward. A servant leader will
overlook being overlooked.

A servant leader is willing to take on all the
responsibility of leadership without taking all
the rights of leadership.

A servant leader is willing to take the blame without taking all the praise. A sure sign of a servant leader is that they are willing to pass on the praise to someone else.

A servant leader is willing to help others get to the top without feeling jealous.

A servant leader is willing to serve without being served. (Matthew 10:28) "The measure of a leader is not the number of people who serve the leader, but the number of people served by the leader." —John C. Maxwell.

A servant leader is willing to be under the authority and accountability of another leader without reservation or reluctance.

A servant leader is willing to hold authority without holding it over people. (Matthew 20:25-26; 1 Peter 5:2, 3)

A servant leader is willing to look out for what's best for the group without looking out for what's best for themselves. A servant leader is not out to attain personal gain. He is always looking out for what is best for the rest.

A servant leader is always ready to listen without feeling he must speak. (James 1:19)

A servant leader is willing to delegate to others without being demanding of others. If you only delegate to others what you don't like to do as a leader, there is a good chance you're not a servant leader.

A servant leader is willing to demonstrate by example without drawing attention to themselves. When a servant leader leads by example, it's not for a photo op.

A servant leader will not demand from others without first demanding from themselves. They exemplify their own expectations. "A godly leader finds strength by realizing his weakness, finds authority by being under authority, finds direction by laying down his own plans, finds vision by seeing the needs of others, finds credibility by being an example, finds loyalty by expressing compassion, finds honor by being faithful, finds greatness by being a servant."
—Roy Lessin

"We must serve before we can lead."
   —William Arthur Ward

"Whatever our career may be, true leadership
   means to receive power from God and to use it
   under God's rule to serve people in God's way."
   —Leighton Ford

"Servant leadership is all about making the goals
   clear and then rolling your sleeves up and doing
   whatever it takes to help people win. In that
   situation, they don't work for you; you work for
   them." —Ken Blanchard

"A good leader takes more than his share of the
   blame and less than his share of the credit."
   —John C. Maxwell

"It is amazing what you can accomplish if you do
   not care who gets the credit."
   —Harry S. Truman

"The best way to tell if someone is a servant leader
   is to watch how they react when they are
   treated like one." —Sam Molind

4 Necessary Ingredients for Untangling Problems (Daniel 5:12):

1. Knowledge (wisdom)
2. Good judgment
3. The Spirit of God to lead and guide you
4. The ability to interpret what is happening and why. (Rules of interpretation must be applied.)

22 Simple Rules to Help You Untangle Your Problems:

1. Don't deal with a problem without first taking the time to kneel in prayer about it. (Philippians 4:6; 1 Samuel 1:15-16)

2. Don't confuse a problem with a different point of view.
   - Unity and uniformity are NOT the same thing.
   - Just because it's different from your perspective does not mean it's wrong. (Philippians 3:15-16)

3. Don't point out problems without sharing some positive points as well. You will negate your

influence with others if you are continually negative. Balance criticism with a compliment when possible.

4. Don't point out problems that are pointless or petty. It's like the challenge flag in football. You only get so many in the game. If you mismanage your challenge, you may be without a challenge when you really need one.

5. Don't make judgments on problems that are outside of your jurisdiction.

6. Don't harp on a problem when you are unwilling to help. (Matthew 23:4) Before you jump on a problem to point it out, ask yourself, "Am I willing to get involved to help solve?" If not, leave the problem alone.

7. Don't point out a problem unless you are prepared to provide a potential or possible solution. This would eliminate a tremendous amount of criticism.

8. Don't waste your time complaining about a problem when you are unwilling to change your current course of action.

- Sometimes a situation requires a new solution.

- "The definition of insanity is doing the same thing and expecting a different outcome." —Albert Einstein

9. Don't go public with a problem until you have communicated privately with the person who caused the problem or who has the authority to resolve the problem. (Matthew 18:15-16)

10. Don't listen to a complaint from someone who has not already confronted the person directly involved or responsible. Every time someone comes to you about a complaint or problem, ask them, "Have you talked to....?"

11. Don't execute someone for a problem while making excuses for yourself regarding the same issue. (Matthew 7:3-5)

12. Don't force a new problem while attempting to fix an old problem.

    - Changing direction does not fix anything unless you are going to the right destination.

- If you have the wrong address plugged into your GPS, it does not matter how many times you change direction or turn; you'll never get to where you need to be.

13. Don't take sides regarding a problem unless you have witnessed it firsthand or gathered enough secondhand information from both sides of the situation. When you hear one side of the story, you know part of the story; when you hear both sides of the story, you still only know part of the story.

   - "The first one to plead his cause seems right, Until his neighbor comes and examines him." (Proverbs 18:17, NKJV)

14. Don't wait until it's too late to point out information regarding a problem.

   - Leaders learn to anticipate in advance potential problems. Whenever it's possible, resolve potential problems before they evolve. Leaders learn to gauge "problem probability." Many problems could be solved with preventative care.

15. Don't try to resolve a problem before you research and understand all the dynamics of

the problem. There may be a good reason why the situation is being handled that way.

16. Don't deal with a problem without consulting someone in authority within your organization. Your ideas are welcome, but don't implement them without first seeking approval.

17. Don't think you can solve a huge problem without gathering the smartest and wisest people you know to think it through. (Acts 6:3)

18. Don't buy into thinking that a tough problem can be completely solved with an easy decision or simple solution. Most decisions, especially regarding difficult problems, don't come with an easy button. In fact, sometimes to solve the most difficult problems, you must make some of the most difficult leadership decisions of your life.

19. Don't rely on a policy to prevent all your problems. While policies and procedures are essential to organizational health, they will not eliminate all your ongoing problems. Too often we like to create a policy rather than communicate and deal with the person who is causing the problem.

20. Don't continue to give your attention to a problem that has already been addressed unless the problem is not fixed.

21. Don't forget to provide encouragement as you encounter progress in solving a problem. (Ephesians 4:29)

22. Don't get caught up in secondary issues when a primary problem needs to be pursued and addressed. Deal with root problems, not fruit problems.

Managing Your Mistakes

Do you ever make mistakes? If you don't think so, you are MISTAKEN!

A mistake is a temporary setback where a comeback is still possible. A failure is a repeated mistake that was left untreated.

"Failure is not a single, cataclysmic event. You don't fail overnight. Instead, failure is a few errors in judgment, repeated every day." —Jim Rohn

When it comes to mistakes,

1. You can attempt to avoid them, but don't allow yourself to be paranoid because of them.
   • "If you're not making mistakes, then you're not doing anything. I'm positive that a doer makes mistakes." —John Wooden

2. Expect them, but don't excuse them. As a general rule, don't overlook or overreact to them.

3. Admit them when they happen, but don't try to omit the responsibility that comes along with committing them.
   • "A man must be big enough to admit his mistakes, smart enough to profit from them,

and strong enough to correct them."
—John C. Maxwell

- "Sometimes when you innovate, you make mistakes. It is best to admit them quickly and get on with improving your other innovations." —Steve Jobs

4. Autograph them, but don't telegraph them. An autograph is your signature. When you make a mistake, you need to own it. A good leader will initial their mistakes and move on without making a big deal.

- My sixth-grade chorus teacher used to say, "If you are going to make a mistake, do it with confidence."

5. Recognize your mistakes, but don't agonize over them forever. A mistake should refine you, not define you.

6. Review them, but don't regularly repeat them. One of the reasons we often repeat our mistakes is we don't review them to investigate.

7. Be quick to correct them, but don't fail to connect what you can learn from them.

- Don't miss an opportunity to connect the dots with your mistake. Don't correct the result without correcting the reason for the mistake.

- "The successful man will profit from his mistakes and try again in a different way." —Dale Carnegie
- "It isn't making mistakes that's critical; it's correcting them and getting on with the principal task." —Donald Rumsfeld

8. Understand the potential risk involved, but don't undertake them recklessly. There is a difference between calculated risks and careless risks.

9. Be patient when you make mistakes, and don't punish someone else when they make the same mistakes.

10. Information is important, but don't limit your education to your own experiences.

As a leader, you will choose to be either teachable or untouchable when it comes to your mistakes. That choice will determine your ultimate success.

"Failure is good; it's fertilizer. Everything I've learned about coaching, I've learned from making mistakes." —Rick Pitino

FAIL = First Attempt In Learning

"I have not failed. I've just found 10,000 ways that won't work." —Thomas Edison

"Success is not final; failure is not fatal. It is the courage to continue that counts."
—Winston Churchill

"Success is going from failure to failure without loss of enthusiasm."
—Winston Churchill

"Only those who dare to fail greatly can ever achieve greatly." —Robert F. Kennedy

"It is impossible to live without failing at something unless you live so cautiously that you might as well not have lived at all, in which case you have failed by default."
—J. K. Rowling

"Failure isn't fatal, but failure to change might be." —John Wooden

"Failure is information. We label it failure, but it is more like, 'This didn't work, and I'm a problem solver, so I'll try something else.'" —Carol Dweck

Leading a Meeting

No matter what you do in life, you will likely find yourself in a place where you need to be leading a meeting. If you serve on a committee, you are either contributing or contaminating.

I hope you take your role seriously. Most people serve for the honor of being on a committee, not to help.

When it comes to meetings, inexperienced leaders often lack:
- Exposure (to how a meeting should be properly run)
- Experience (sitting in a well-led meeting)
- Expertise (in handling difficult situations that arise in a meeting)
- Expectation (of how an effective meeting should be managed)

Being elected to a leadership board will not automatically make you effective in that leadership position without training.

If you have any experience in leadership, you know that often a meeting can be defeating!

It is the leader's responsibility to MODEL what a meeting looks like. In order to accomplish that, we must understand some basics about leading a meeting. The leader of a meeting is like the conductor of an orchestra. The conductor:

- Prepares the group
- Chooses the music
- Calls everyone to order
- Starts the music
- Sets the tempo
- Pulls out the different parts
- Continues to direct
- Ends the piece
- Gives credit to the orchestra

Having the right people in the orchestra makes all the difference in the world. Think about the last junior high orchestra you heard, then compare that to the New York Philharmonic.

More on Leading a Meeting:

1. It is essential to establish expectations in advance.
   - Regular time and location of your meetings
   - The purpose of the team
   - Attendance at meetings
   - The duration of the meeting

- How the team will govern itself (<u>Robert's Rules of Order</u>, by consensus)
- The boundaries and authority of the team
- Communication of expectations (what team members need to bring to the meeting)

2. The most important aspect of any meeting is preparation by the person leading the meeting. Never walk into a meeting without designing the purpose of the meeting and detailing plans for team members. A meeting can be ruined without gathering proper information for decisions to be made. Do your homework!
   - The less frequently you meet, the more you need to prepare for the meeting.

3. When you are leading a meeting, never show up on time or late. Always be 15-20 minutes early to unlock the door, set up the room, and be ready to start on time.
   - There are too many unknown variables that can develop and delay your meeting. Utilizing technology is wonderful, but it takes time to manage effectively.

4. Start and end your meeting on schedule. Don't wait on those who are late before starting.

   - Don't let people who miss meetings monopolize the next meeting by trying to get caught up on what they missed. When a person misses a meeting, it is the responsibility of the person who was absent to find out what he or she missed.
   - It's okay to end a meeting without being finished. Start the next meeting where you left off.
   - "Then the meeting broke up, and everybody went home." (John 7:53, NLT)

5. Have a prepared agenda in advance of the meeting outlining the purpose, objectives, and goals of the meeting. Use your agenda as a communication device. A meeting without an agenda is like a journey without a map.

   - Invite others to suggest agenda items prior to the meeting. Check in at the beginning of the meeting to confirm the agenda and to solicit priorities for the group (Start with the end in mind. What do we want to accomplish by the time this meeting ends?)
   - Announce what a successful meeting will look like in advance. (If we accomplish these objectives, it will be a good meeting.)

- Don't be overly aggressive with your agenda. There is great satisfaction when you can act on the few items accomplished on your agenda.
- Prepare an appropriate agenda based on:
  - The length of the meeting (how long you will be meeting)
  - The breadth and depth of the subject(s) being discussed at the meeting
  - The urgency of the decisions at hand
  - Who will be in attendance (If you find out most of your team is going to be absent, it may not be the best time to make major decisions.)
  - How long it will be before your next meeting (or how often you will meet)

6. Solicit input from each team member before deciding. Let everyone give their input and then decide. Encourage candor in your communication with one another.
   - It is a good rule of thumb for the chairperson not to share his opinion first. It may hinder people from sharing their true opinions. The person leading the meeting can either spur on discussion or squelch it.

- When the leader of a group postpones giving his opinion, he does not sway the decision-making process.
- A leader will debilitate the meeting if he does not facilitate the meeting.

7. Keep things moving. Don't allow a topic to be discussed to death. Your team will respect you if you respect their time. Never prolong when you can move along.
   - Suggestions:
     - Move on from decisions that have already been made or determined.
     - Move on from consensus.
     - Move on from trivial discussions.
     - Move on from discussions that only affect a few team members.
     - Move on from discussions where the team has no authority to make change.
     - Move on from divisive discussions (dissension).
   - A leader is responsible to intervene in interruptions of the meeting.
   - If you're prepared and give enough information in advance, you can advance your agenda farther.
   - Surveys show that companies waste almost 20% of their payroll on bad meetings.

8. Forward progress! Meetings can often be two steps forward and three steps back. Don't keep going over issues that have already been decided by the team. Review, but do not rewind all the way to the beginning.

9. The meeting fails when there are too many details discussed. Focus on the big picture. Deal with necessary details, and delegate and report on the rest in written form. Don't take up meeting time with unnecessary information that can be passed on in written form. Include a section on the agenda called, "For your information." Ask meeting attendees to read it on their own time and let you know if they have questions.

10. When making decisions, if there is not consensus, lay the issue aside until more information can be gained. Don't drag it out. Sometimes you need to just have the group go home and pray about it and sleep on it.

11. Don't allow team members to hijack the agenda. When the discussion is going off track, pull it back in. When things come up that are not on the table, take good notes and tell the person, "We'll come back to that later." It is important to keep track of items

that come up that need to be discussed at the next meeting.

- As a leader, don't be afraid to interrupt an interruption.

12. Have someone on your team taking good notes/minutes and then keep them somewhere on file. In addition to keeping good notes, it is good to email minutes to your team members. Make sure all decisions and discussions are well documented.

- Document what was delegated, along with the deadline. Document details for the next meeting.
- James Kirk said, "A meeting is an event where minutes are taken and hours are wasted."

13. Remember the rules for delegation:

- What gets delegated with a deadline gets done.
- What gets checked gets done (follow-up).
- What gets rewarded gets done (acknowledged).
- Make assignments and expect action on them.

14. Confidentiality is critical. It is important to challenge—and chastise, if necessary—people in confidentiality. What is communicated in the room must stay in the room!
    - Call any confidentiality breaches on the carpet immediately.

15. Review and recap anything that was decided, delegated, or even discussed that will be delayed until the next meeting. End the meeting with a summary of what was accomplished as well as any action items. Without this, participants may fail to recognize the benefits of meeting.
    - Never end the meeting without first determining the date of the next meeting.

10 Simple Rules for People Who Lead Meetings:

1. Do not get in the habit of canceling regularly scheduled meetings because of your own scheduling conflicts.

2. Do not extend a meeting longer than is necessary. It's okay to let people out early if you have completed your agenda.

3. If you cannot personally attend a meeting, make sure you appoint someone to lead it. You must give someone authority to lead and then

let the team know you have empowered that person.

4. Do not allow your team to get in a creative rut. Rearrange the meeting room, go to a different room, or change the style of presentation just to keep things fresh. Shuffle things up a bit to keep the team interested.

5. Don't be afraid of debate, dialogue, and difference of opinion within a meeting.

6. Don't be afraid to solicit feedback from team members on how your meetings are going. Don't be afraid to make adjustments and accept suggestions that will make the meeting more productive.

7. Don't hold meetings outside the meeting.

8. Don't let your team get in the habit of pointing out problems without pointing toward solutions to those problems.

9. Don't keep rehashing a decision once it has been reached.

10. Don't be discouraged if things are not dramatically different at the next meeting. It takes time to train and rein in a meeting.

Leadership Advice to Give You a Leadership Advantage

Leaders don't hold on to what they have found helpful; they pass it on to others.

Develop a DO LIST each day and then DO IT. There is no advantage to making a list you do not act on. Once you make your list, avoid procrastination. No one ever reaches their destination through procrastination.

- The NIKE principle: do it now.
- Consider moving your do list to your calendar, with specific time commitments.

Learn how to manage your time wisely. Develop a reputation for being ON TIME. Develop a punctuality mentality.

- On time is 15 minutes early.
- If you're on time, you're late.
- Nothing says, "I value you and your time" like showing up early so you can start on time.
- "Being early is being on time, being on time is being late, and being late is unacceptable."
  —Eric Jerome Dickey

Take time to develop systems that make you successful. The earlier you develop these systems, the more effective and productive they will be.

Give as much attention to substance as you do to appearance. Appearance can gain attention, but only substance will retain it.

Acknowledge and answer emails, phone calls, and other communications in a timely manner. Nothing reveals responsibility like responding to communications within a reasonable period.

- If you can't answer communications immediately, at least acknowledge them immediately. Let the sender know when you can address their need.

You can never underestimate the net worth of a good network. Be careful to be a bridge builder rather than a bridge burner.

Never go anywhere without a notebook. Get in the habit of writing ideas, insights, and information down immediately. Record it, and it will be remembered. A voice recorder can serve the same purpose. Use your mobile phone to capture thoughts in real time.

Meet—and if possible, beat—due dates and deadlines. Don't let delinquency define your leadership. Being late is not a great leadership quality.

Develop a personal growth plan. Be intentional about ways you intend to grow as a leader. Leaders grow systematically, not automatically. Set up a system to grow daily.
- Hire a credentialed leadership coach who can facilitate and accelerate your personal growth as a leader.

Show genuine appreciation and say thank you for everything. Gratitude is an attractive attitude in leadership.

Lead with the same standard and intensity regardless of the size of leadership opportunity. Take seriously every assignment or task. (Luke 16:10; Luke 19:17)

Keep your office and desk clean. A cluttered desk is a good indication of a disorganized leader. Your office space is a place where people get a preview of your organizational skills.

Always seek the advice and counsel of wise and trusted leaders before you advance a decision. (Proverbs 11:14; Proverbs 15:22; Proverbs 24:6)

Evaluate everything you do. Look for ways to improve it or remove it.

- Build time into your day to reflect. The practice of reflecting and evaluating is key to improving.

Exceed expectations. Go the extra mile. There is not a lot of traffic on this road. Too many leaders have developed the habit of doing just enough to get by.

- "Those who take the high road of humility in Washington, DC are not bothered by heavy traffic." —Allen Simpson in a eulogy for George H. W. Bush

Whatever you do, do with excellence. (Colossians 3:23)

Keep your word. There's too much at stake when you break a promise. Don't promise what you cannot perform.

Persistence pays off. Sometimes endurance is more important than expertise.

- "Never, never, never give up." —Winston Churchill
- "Most of the important things in the world have been accomplished by people who kept on trying when there seemed to be no hope at all."—Dale Carnegie

- "Nothing in this world can take the place of persistence. Talent will not; nothing is more com-mon than unsuccessful people with talent. Genius will not; unrewarded genius is almost a proverb. Education will not; the world is full of educated derelicts. Persistence and determination alone are omnipotent. The slogan 'press on' has solved, and always will solve, the problems of the human race." — Calvin Coolidge
- "Never let formal education get in the way of your learning." —Mark Twain

Take full responsibility for what happens in your life today. Don't pout, point the finger, or pretend it never happened. Be quick to admit your mistakes and faults. Fess up when you mess up.

Great things can be accomplished through prayer and taking the time to prepare (preprayer and praypare); don't omit either one. There is less to repair when you take the time to prepare. Main-tain a dedication to preparation.

- "There are no secrets to success. It is the result of preparation, hard work, and learning from failure." —Colin Powell

Walk in humility. Be humble so you don't stumble. Pride goes before a fall. (Proverbs 22:4; James 4:6)
- "Humility is not thinking less of yourself; it's thinking of yourself less." —C. S. Lewis

Yearn to learn more. Seek out opportunities to grow in your leadership abilities. When you stop learning, you stop leading. No matter how much you know, there is still room to grow.
- Leaders are learners, and leaders are readers.

The **SAID** acronym for reading by Michael Hyatt:
S = Stimulation
A = Assimilation
I = Innovation
D = Dissemination

Guard your reputation; it takes a lifetime to build and only a moment to destroy. Build boundaries into your life. Don't avoid accountability. (Acts 6:3; 1 Timothy 3:7; Proverbs 22:1; Proverbs 3:3-4)

Never assume. Always follow up and follow through; it will save you hours of frustration.

Maintain a proper respect and response to authority. If you can't honor authority, you can't hold authority. (Romans 13:1-3)

Leaders Who Lead Well

Leaders who lead well:

- Dedicate meaningful time with individual members of their team. Your team not only needs access to you but excess time with you. Give quality time and quantity time.

- Concentrate their attention and emotion on the big-picture mission.

- Orchestrate an environment of excellence. Leaders who lead well are conductors of the culture of excellence. They orchestrate the environment where excellence is expected, inspected, corrected, and perfected.

- Incorporate individual values into their organizational vision.

- Participate personally in organizational expectations. Don't ask others to do what they are not willing to do. Lead by example, not by expectation! Leadership really is SHOW AND TELL.
  - Also, TELL AND SHOW. The audio and the video must match.
  - Organizationally, the hangings on the walls must match the happenings in the halls.

- Anticipate potential problems and possible opportunities prior to reality. Don't wait to swerve until you crash. Make adjustments in advance.

- Collaborate, rather than dominate, the decision-making process.

- Debate issues effectively without deflating individuals. Disagreements don't have to be disastrous.

- Welcome, even invite, oppositional views and perspectives.

- Instigate protocol, policies, and procedures that improve overall health of the organization.

- Delegate authority with responsibility to those who possess ability to progress a process. They don't seek power; they empower.

- One of the greatest disservices and sources of frustration is to delegate responsibility without simultaneously granting authority.
  o "Surround yourself with the best people you can find, delegate authority, and don't interfere as long as the policy you've decided upon is being carried out." —Ronald Reagan

- Communicate intentionally, insightfully, and instantly with as many people as possible. The forms of communication change, but the formula does not. The formula is: Leadership + Communication = Success.

- Facilitate the type of change necessary as well as the timing and timetable of change. There are leaders who are fascinated by change but never facilitate it.

- Generate an atmosphere of innovation and creativity where leaders can debate ideas and not be demonized or demoralized by their thoughts.

- Separate critique from criticism. Learn to discern the difference between criticism that is ridiculous and a critique that is reasonable.

- Accelerate to safe speed within the organizational culture.

- Celebrate and appreciate individual and corporate accomplishments.

- Calculate the risk vs. reward before instigating any new ideas.

- Captivate the spirit of the team with ongoing inspiration and insight to the shared vision.

- Translate reality into insightful information.

- Educate continually through new information that will enable them to lead more effectively and efficiently.

Building a Foundation for Delegation

Delegation is the transfer of responsibility for the performance of a task from one individual to another while retaining accountability for the outcome.

Always delegate the priority when you delegate the project. Determine the timetable when you deal out the task. Every delegated task should have a deadline.

Disclose all the details when you delegate. Set clear expectations. There should be no small print. Be upfront with your expectations.

Document anything you delegate in writing. Give everyone involved a copy.

Discuss up front how success will be determined and evaluated.

Determine who the person with a delegated task will direct report to.

Divvy specific portions of the project to be assigned to specific people on the project and let them work at their own pace.

Don't double-delegate. (Don't assign two different people the same task.)

Leaders who are effective at delegating teach people how to do things as well as tell them what to do.

Reject reverse-delegation (when something delegated ends up coming back to you to finish).

Understand the difference between delegation and dumping. One is fruitful; the other is frustrating.

The difference between delegating and dumping is determined by how long it takes to get routed.

Don't get in the habit of only delegating to others what you dislike or don't want to do; that's demoralizing.

Don't forget to delegate authority when you delegate an assignment. Keep in mind, however, that you can delegate authority, but you cannot delegate responsibility.

Once you have outlined any important instructions, don't interfere with the process unless you are asked.

"The best executive is the one who has sense enough to pick good men to do what he wants done, and self-restraint enough to keep from meddling with them while they do it."
—Theodore Roosevelt.

Understand up front that when you delegate something to someone, it may be done differently than you would have done it.

Be careful not to disrupt or discourage the delegation process with critical comments. A supervisor needs to be more of a cheerleader than a critic.

Never assume that because you delegated it, it's getting done.

Be careful not to be delinquent in what you have delegated. Follow up and follow through. Reward or reprimand.

Don't continue to delegate a job to someone who misses deadlines, mismanages tasks, or falls short of your standard of expectation and excellence.

Learn to delegate something small before you risk delegating something substantial. (Matthew 13:12) Let them prove what they can perform in incremental responsibilities.

Treat the people you delegate well, or you may be looking for someone different to share the load down the road.

"Never tell people how to do things. Tell them what to do, and they will surprise you with their ingenuity." —George S. Patton

"Delegating work works, provided the one delegating works too." —Robert Half

Dealing with Criticism

I made 5 mistakes early in my leadership:

1. I believed if I was doing what was right, I would not be criticized.
2. I believed if I was doing a good job at what I was doing, I would not be criticized.
3. I believed if I went to another place of leadership, they would appreciate me more and criticize me less.
4. I believed the more experience I had, the less I would be criticized.
5. I believed people who were on my side would compliment me more than criticize me.

Great leaders must learn to deal with an absurd amount of criticism.

3 Types of Criticism:

1. Nonproductive criticism (no benefit or point to it)
2. Destructive criticism
   - Usually told to others, not the person being criticized
   - Done so poorly that any valid point becomes invalid

140

- Criticism can be:
  - Unkind
  - Unfair
  - Undeserving
  - Unsubstantial
  - Untrue
  - Undermining
  - UnChristlike
  - Unsanctified

3. Instructive criticism (teaching behind)
   - Some call this constructive criticism. The problem is, constructive usually is when I criticize you; destructive is when you criticize me.
   - It is done in a spirit of humility and honesty.

As a leader, you need to be on the lookout for a mentor who will speak into your life with candor.

A leader should expect to be the object of criticism. Criticism is the sales tax of success. The more you succeed, the more you can expect to be taxed.

Always explore criticism before you ignore criticism. Don't write it off before you determine if it's accurate. Carefully review to see if it's true. Take time to analyze when you've been criticized. (Proverbs 13:18)

Never fear criticism when you're right; never ignore it when you're wrong.

Don't take every comment that comes your way as a criticism. (Romans 15:15). A leader must strike the balance between being insensitive and being hypersensitive. A leader sometimes needs to be compassionately calloused.

Acquire information and insight before you fire back. Research and reflect on the matter before you respond. It is always a good idea to calm down before you come back.

Take action on the problem being criticized, not the person doing the criticizing. Act—don't attack.

Carefully review repetitive criticisms, especially when they come from different sources. When you receive criticism from multiple sources, you need to pay attention.

The outcome will usually depend on how you defend yourself regarding the criticism. The end will depend on how you defend yourself. When your reaction is intensive and defensive, it becomes offensive.

A critical blow can be an indicator of something deeper, below the surface. There is usually more substance below the surface. Drill deeper, and you will discover oil.

Quickly forgive, or you will constantly relive the criticism. You can't always solve the issue, but you can settle it in your heart.

Realize that the critical can often be hypocritical. (Matthew 23:4)

Leaders must learn to rise above those who criticize. It's critical that we learn how to manage criticism.

Tips on Responding to Criticism:

- Take the criticism to God in prayer immediately.
- Do not respond immediately.
- Separate facts from feelings.
- Share with a trusted friend who will give godly counsel.
- Take yourself out of the situation.
- Write out your response.
- Be careful not to be defensive.
- Teach your people the proper way to give criticism.
- Don't criticize without a solution.
- Don't criticize without signing your name. ("Anonymous" means nothing.)
- Don't criticize in the hallway. (Set an appointment to talk together.)
- Learn from it, and let it go.

"Criticism may not be agreeable, but it is necessary. It fulfils the same function as pain in the human body. It calls attention to an unhealthy state of things." —Winston Churchill

Never assume that because criticism is being made, a correction must be made. Sometimes your loudest critics will attack you when you are going in the right direction.

Criticism is always difficult to accept, but if we receive it with humility and a desire to improve our character, it can be very helpful. Only a fool does not profit when he is rebuked for his mistakes.

"You can't let praise or criticism get to you. It's a weakness to get caught up in either one." —John Wooden.

"The trouble with most of us is that we would rather be ruined by praise than saved by criticism." —Norman Vincent Peale

"The way we respond to criticism pretty much depends on the way we respond to praise. If praise humbles us, then criticism will build us up. But if praise inflates us, then criticism will crush us. Both responses lead to our defeat." —Warren W. Wiersbe

Leadership Beatitudes

BLESSED are leaders who seek to please the Lord and not the crowd (Ephesians 6:6; Galatians 1:10), for they shall be pleasing to God.

BLESSED are leaders willing to make personal sacrifices to accomplish God's will and purpose in the organizations they lead (Romans 12:1-2), for they shall be satisfied.

BLESSED are leaders who regularly spend time alone with the Lord (Luke 5:16), for they shall not burn out!

BLESSED are leaders whose affirmation comes from the praise of God (Matthew 25:21) rather than the praise of men. (John 12:43)

BLESSED are leaders who seek wisdom rather than wealth (1 Kings 3:9), for they shall be rich.

BLESSED are leaders who have purposed in their hearts not to defile themselves with anything that could damage their character or the reputation of the organizations they lead (Daniel 1:8), for they shall escape scandal.

BLESSED are leaders who are following while they are leading (1 Corinthians 11:1), for they shall not get lost.

BLESSED are leaders who walk by faith, not by FEAR (2 Corinthians 5:7), for they shall be pleasing to God. (Hebrews 11:6)

BLESSED are leaders who understand the times and seek God to know just what to do (1 Chronicles 12:32), for they shall receive guidance.

BLESSED are leaders who lean on the Lord instead of their own understanding (Proverbs 3:5-6), for they shall not be made out to be a fool.

BLESSED are leaders who lead by example (Philippians 3:17), for they will multiply their followers.

BLESSED are leaders who follow up and follow through on what they say they will do, for they shall make a difference.

BLESSED are leaders who stay humble instead of being humbled (James 4:6-10), for they shall be exalted. (1 Peter 5:5-6)

BLESSED are leaders with a pioneering spirit who are never satisfied, for they shall conquer the land.

BLESSED are leaders who are in touch with the people they lead, for they shall not be left walking alone.

BLESSED are leaders who are teaching and training and motivating others to lead (1 Timothy 6:12), for they shall leave a legacy.

BLESSED are leaders who know the purpose behind why they are leading and make it a priority, for they shall not get sidetracked.

BLESSED are leaders who manage their own families well (1 Timothy 3:4), for they shall find lasting joy and fulfillment.

BLESSED are leaders who are actively, aggressively attempting to reach people instead of spending all their time in the management of the church, for they shall never lose their zeal.

BLESSED are leaders who enjoy what they are doing, for they shall truly find fulfillment.

BLESSED are leaders who continually learn and grow, for they shall keep the organization growing.

BLESSED are leaders who continually model change, for they shall not become outdated.

BLESSED are leaders who speak the truth in love (Ephesians 4:15), for they shall prove they are His disciples. (John 13:35)

BLESSED are leaders who care enough to confront (Galatians 2:11; Hebrews 12:5) for they shall be respected and resolve conflict.

BLESSED are leaders who wait on the Lord (Proverbs 3:5-6), for they shall find out that it was worth it. (Isaiah 40:31)

Leading with Excellence

Excellence is something that is easy to pick out but harder to put out.

"Excellence is taking every assignment seriously for the glory of God." —Kent Crockett

4 Ways to Achieve Excellence:

1. Lose the excuses. Excuses do not exempt you from striving for excellence, so lose them!
2. Choose to excel at excellence. It's hard to lead well if you have not made excellence a key factor in your leadership development.
3. Infuse a spirit of excellence into everything you do.
   - Colin Powell said, "If you are going to achieve excellence in big things, you develop the habit in little matters."
4. Refuse to compromise the bar of excellence. Once you SET the expectation of excellence, let that be your leadership measuring stick.

Reviews are necessary! Leaders obtain and maintain excellence through constant evaluation and expectation. You must patrol your goal.

Everything God did was excellent. (Genesis 1:31) Even His name means excellence. "O LORD, our Lord, How excellent is Your name in all the earth!" (Psalm 8:1, 9, NKJV)

Daniel distinguished himself above the governors and satraps because an excellent spirit was in him. (Daniel 5:12, 14)

Excellence distinguishes an extraordinary leader from an ordinary leader. If you want to distinguish yourself among others, develop and display a spirit of excellence in everything you do.

Paul challenges us to do 2 things:
1. Approve things that are excellent. (Philippians 1:10, Romans 2:18)
2. Think about things that are excellent. (Philippians 4:8)

Someone once said, "Every job is a self-portrait of the person who did it. So autograph your work with excellence."

Hanging in my office is a plaque that influences my actions every day. It reads, "Excellence: If it's worth doing, it's worth doing well."

Servant leaders can achieve a higher standard of excellence in everything they do because they believe they are serving a higher purpose than themselves.

"The quality of a person's life is in direct proportion to their commitment to excellence regardless of their chosen endeavor."
—Vince Lombardi

Excellence gives a leader the competitive advantage.

10 Requirements on the Road to Excellence:

1. Be exposed to excellence. You must be exposed to excellence before you can set your standard of excellence.
    - When you SEE excellence in action, you can SET a higher standard of excellence. SIGHT is the best INSIGHT into excellence.

2. Understand the expense of excellence.
    - "Excellence can be obtained if you care more than others think is wise, risk more than others think is safe, dream more than others think is practical, expect more than others think is possible, and spend more than others think is reasonable." —Anonymous

- Excellence requires a little more time, a little more energy, a little more money, a little more patience, a little more creativity, a little more effort, but in the final analysis, it's worth it.

3. Set the example of excellence for others. A leader must exhibit it before he can expect it. Excellence starts with the executive.

4. Communicate the expectation of excellence clearly. You must not only set what you expect but explain why excellence is so important to you and the organization.
   - Never assume that excellence will be the outcome if excellence was not involved in the input.

5. Eliminate the excuses of excellence. Excellence requires extra effort, and most people are not willing to pay that price.

6. Master the execution of excellence. Excellence is an attitude, but it is also an action. Autograph your work with excellence.

7. Go through the examination of excellence. Evaluate the level of your excellence.

- "Good, better, best; never let it rest till your good is better and your better is best." —St. Jerome
- You will never, never, never, never hit a higher standard of excellence without the process of evaluation. You must patrol your goal.

8. Create an excitement for excellence. There is something electrifying about the exhibition of excellence.

9. Develop the expansion of excellence. Improvement can be defined as the expansion of excellence. We sometimes focus more on the development of new things while we neglect improving the things we are already doing.

10. Practice extreme excellence. The difference between ordinary and extraordinary is a little extra. Eliminate the "it's good enough" mentality. Excellence is going beyond expectations. It's what the Bible calls going the extra mile. (Matthew 5:41) Extraordinary excellence is really what closes the deal.

Daniel was known for having an "Excellent Spirit." (Daniel 5:12, 14; 6:3)

"Excellence is a process that should occupy all our days." —Ted Engstrom

7 Things that Threaten the Extinction of Excellence:

1. Throwing things together at the last minute (unwillingness to prepare)
2. Failing to evaluate everything you do and keep good notes
3. Mediocre mentality
4. Fear of hurting someone's feelings (lack of honest feedback)
5. Satisfaction with better rather than striving for best (settling rather than stretching)
6. Failure to challenge the process
7. No clear, measurable markers

"Excellence means matching your practice with your potential." —Paul Borthwick

"Excellence is a better teacher than mediocrity. The lessons of the ordinary are everywhere. Truly profound and original insights are to be found only in studying the exemplary."
—Warren G. Bennis

"Perfection is not attainable, but if we chase perfection, we can catch excellence."
—Vince Lombardi

Leadership Myth Busters

A leadership myth is something we have been taught, trained, or told that does not hold up under the examination of experience.

Myth   A great title is vital to be able to lead.
Truth   A title is not a necessity for a true leader.

Myth   You must be in charge to effectively lead change.
Truth   You can effectively influence change from any level.

Myth   Born leaders make better leaders.
Truth   Leadership can be learned.

Myth   Every person has the potential to be a great leader.
Truth   Some people are just not designed for leadership.

Myth   The grass is greener on the other side.
Truth   Every setting has its setbacks.

Myth	Money and moving up the ladder are always the great motivators of leaders.
Truth	Lack of adequate compensation is a demotivator, but leaders are motivated by their vision and passions.
Myth	When things are going well, you can tell there is a good leader at the top.
Truth	There is a good leader in charge somewhere in the organization—not necessarily at the top.
Myth	Bigger is better.
Truth	Better is better.
Myth	If it worked before, it will work again. Likewise, if it worked there, it will work here.
Truth	Current success is not always a clear indicator of future success. There are many external factors that differ and will affect the outcome. "What got you here won't get you there." —Marshall Goldsmith
Myth	When you promote people, they will perform better and produce more.
Truth	If they are not doing it now, they won't do it then.

Myth	Visionary leaders don't have to deal with details, just the big picture.
Truth	If they don't deal with the details, they won't be leading very long.
Myth	Great leaders possess charismatic and magnetic personalities.
Truth	Some great leaders have little personality at all.
Myth	The person who holds the highest position is the person leading the organization.
Truth	The person with the most influence is leading the group.
Myth	Education is the best preparation for a leadership position.
Truth	More education does not necessarily mean more wisdom. And while education is important, it is evaluated experience that makes the ultimate difference.
Myth	Leadership gets easier with more experience.
Truth	The higher you go in leadership, the harder it gets, no matter how much experience you have.

Myth	The leader knows it all and has all the answers.
Truth	The leader knows who knows. A leader cannot have a complete knowledge of everything. That is why he must have the right people with the right skills on his team.
Myth	Your personal life has no direct impact on your professional life.
Truth	The two are intimately intertwined.
Myth	No one is irreplaceable.
Truth	It would be irresponsible to lose a key player in your organization.
Myth	Your age can limit your advancement.
Truth	Your actions, accomplishments, and attitudes determine your future.
Myth	The person with the best qualifications gets the job.
Truth	The person with the best connections or who makes the best impression gets the job.

Myth   Leaders must be loud and demanding to
       get people's attention.
Truth You don't have to be mean to mean
       business.

Myth   It's lonely at the top.
Truth Effective leaders will surround
       themselves with a great team.

The Kind of Leaders I'm Looking For

Leaders who lead with honesty, character, and integrity.

Leaders who manage their day with an organizational system.

Leaders who are team players.

Leaders who understand their job and the role they play on the team.

Leaders who are on time, on task, and on target.

Leaders who make forward progress and accomplish things in their area of responsibility.

Leaders who are innovative and creative in their area of responsibility.

Leaders who bring input, ideas, and impressions to the table for consideration.

Leaders who follow up and follow through with responsibilities that have been delegated to them.

Leaders who are candid and caring with their comments and communication.

Leaders who carry their share of the leadership load.

Leaders who evaluate, measure, and improve the effectiveness of their area of responsibility.

Leaders who inquire or seek out information when they are unclear or unsure.

Leaders who work within the systems and structure that have been set up within the organization.

Leaders who take ownership in the organization. They step up to the plate when they see a need.

Leaders who influence decisions through their wise input.

Leaders who think outside the box.

Leaders who step back to see the big picture, not just a snapshot of the vision

Leaders who "take a bullet" for those on their team.

Leaders who look ahead and plan ahead in their
area of responsibility.

Leaders who grow in their own leadership and walk
with Jesus.

Leaders who lead with excellence and enthusiasm.

Leaders who do not point out problems without
pointing toward solutions.

Leaders who are loyal to the leadership, the cause,
and the team.

Leaders who are committed to relationship and
community.

Leaders who function as a family willing to love,
laugh, listen, and let things go.

Leaders who do whatever it takes to get the job
done.

On-Time Leadership

Being on time is not only what makes a good first impression as a leader but makes a lasting impression as well.

A lot of people live by the motto, "Better late than never." I like what George Bernard Shaw said: "Better never than late."

Being on time is "the courtesy of winners," says the super-achieving editor and author Helen Gurley Brown. There is almost no more important rule for professional success, she advises in her book, I'm Wild Again. Unlike IQ, beauty, or athletic skill, being punctual is something you can control.

Although there is a great deal of material being written on time management, there is very little being taught or written on the value of being on time.

Reinstate and reinforce the value of being on time.

"The bad news is time flies. The good news is, you're the pilot." —Michael Altshuler

"Being early is being on time, being on time is being late, and being late is unacceptable."
—Eric Jerome Dickey

3 Things Happen When You're Late:

1. You frustrate those who are waiting on you.

   - Don't set yourself up for failure. Limit your schedule so you limit how often you must be late.
   - If you know you're going to be late, let people know. Don't wait until you're late to let them know.
   - Don't treat being late lightly. It is a serious offense.

2. You communicate something negative to your team.

   - "My time is more important than yours. It is really a respect issue. In other words, you are saying, "I've got more to do than you; that's why I'm late and you're not."
     o If you are in a place of leadership and have people on your team who continually show up late, let me give you this advice: Don't respect the people who are late by starting late; respect the people who are on time by starting on time.

   - "What I'm here for really isn't that important to me; otherwise, I would have been here on time."
     o People will generally communicate that value with one of three actions.

- —Showing up early
- —Showing up just on time
- —Showing up late

- "I'm not leading; I'm being led." When I'm not on time, I'm basically saying, "Something else is in charge of me."
  - "Life offers two great gifts: time and the ability to choose how we spend it. Planning is a process of choosing among those many options. If we do not choose to plan, then we choose to have others plan for us."
    —Richard I. Winword

- "I'm a procrastinator."
  - Most people who see you being late ultimately believe that if you are given a responsibility with a deadline, it will be late too.
  - Being late is a learned behavior. When "late" characterizes your time, it usually describes your tasks as well.

- "I like to make excuses."
  - "We must use time as a tool, not as a crutch." —John F. Kennedy

- "You can't count on me."
  - Even though I told you I would be here on time—

- o "Unfaithfulness in keeping an appointment is an act of clear dishonesty. You might as well borrow a person's money as his time." —Horace Mann
- "I'm about to mess up your time as well."
  - o When you're late, you will eventually make me late too.
  - o I do two things as a leader when you are late:
    - – "I limit my time with you. (If I've scheduled an hour with you, the clock starts when we were scheduled to start, not when you show up.)
    - – I leave. (If you're not going to be on time, I'm going to leave and set up another time.)
- "You don't have to worry about time either."
  - o Leaders have learned how to manage and maximize their time. If you have good leaders on your team and you always show up late or start the meeting late, guess what they are going to do? You guessed it: they are going to utilize that extra time and show up late too.
- "I'm not prepared for this."
  - o If you were, you would have been on time and ready.

- If you're in charge and you're not early, you're late.
- We make too many assumptions in leadership. We think everything will be ready if we show up just on time. (Never assume.)
- Being early not only guarantees you will be on time but also allows time for more to be accomplished, giving you the leadership edge.

3. You deteriorate your leadership edge. Leaders become known by their time zone. When others say things like, "They'll be late to their own funeral," it's not a compliment.

- Time formula for the leadership edge: LEAVE enough time so that you can BE on time for the event to START on time, STAY on time, and END on time.
  - Remember, it is just as much a sign of great leadership to END a meeting on time as it is to START on time.
  - The best way for you to set the expectation in your organization about being on time is for you to set the example.

The #1 Rule in Leadership: Never Assume!

Leadership assumptions can be expensive and embarrassing but also educational. Here are a few lessons I've learned:

NEVER ASSUME you are immune to temptation: you are not.

NEVER ASSUME that because you hold a leadership position, people will automatically follow you. They will only follow you if you are leading. Holding the title of a leader does not equal holding the influence of a leader.

NEVER ASSUME that because you see it, others see it too. "We simply assume that the way we see things is the way they really are or the way they should be. Our attitudes and behaviors grow out of these assumptions."
—Stephen R. Covey

NEVER ASSUME that because someone is sold on your vision, they can sell it to someone else.

NEVER ASSUME that because you don't perceive it, it's not being perceived.

NEVER ASSUME that because you are not hearing any feedback, there is none; it's just not coming back to you.

NEVER ASSUME that because you have a right to do something, you can do it right away. Sometimes you need to wait until your team is on board or certain pieces of the puzzle are in place.

NEVER ASSUME your team will buy in to a decision if they did not have a chance to weigh in on the decision.

NEVER ASSUME it's not your responsibility just because you had nothing to do with it. If it fell under your leadership watch, it's your responsibility.

NEVER ASSUME that because you thought it, others got it. Your team cannot know what you're thinking unless you let them know what you are thinking.

NEVER ASSUME that because it is insignificant in your mind, it is insignificant in the mind of someone else.

NEVER ASSUME that because it needs done, someone else will do it without it being delegated.

NEVER ASSUME that because you delegated it, it no longer demands your attention. A leader must devote time even to tasks that have been delegated to ensure his success.

NEVER ASSUME that because something is set up, it is settled. Always check up and confirm.

NEVER ASSUME that because you fixed a problem, it will not require your attention down the road.

NEVER ASSUME people will prioritize the tasks you have given them unless you specifically spell out the level of urgency. For your team to understand your priority, you must prioritize for them.

NEVER ASSUME that because someone said they will do it, it will get done.

NEVER ASSUME that because someone said it will get done, it will get done the way you want it to get done. Be specific!

NEVER ASSUME things will keep going the way they're going.

NEVER ASSUME that because you understand it, others understand it too. Just because it makes sense to you does not mean it makes sense to someone else.

NEVER ASSUME that because you communicated it, they understood it. Just because you are a good communicator does not mean you are communicating with your people. If they're listening but not learning, you're losing.

NEVER ASSUME that because you have repeated yourself, you're being redundant. Some things, like vision, need to be repeated over and over.

NEVER ASSUME that because you communicated it, they still remember it. Put it in writing or in memo form.

NEVER ASSUME that because you saw it, it's true. Things are not always as they appear. Don't judge by appearances.

NEVER ASSUME that because I feel this way, everyone else does too. My likes and dislikes will not always be representative of everyone else.

NEVER ASSUME people who have everything are happy, and that if you had it all, you would be happy too.

NEVER ASSUME people are behind you. People behind you today may not be there tomorrow. Sometimes people bail who were once on board.

NEVER ASSUME that because you made the right decision, there will not be repercussions from the decision. It's impossible to please everyone. Good decisions can have bad consequences.

NEVER ASSUME an insignificant decision today will not have a significant impact tomorrow.

NEVER ASSUME information you already know is enough to make the best decision. As a leader, get into the practice of verifying before you make a verdict.

NEVER ASSUME information you've received is correct unless you confirm it.

NEVER ASSUME there is not another side of the story you just heard. Balance it before you believe it.

NEVER ASSUME that when you've corrected a person, you've corrected a problem. You must correct the problem too.

NEVER ASSUME that because the decision you made today was the right one, it will be the right one tomorrow. Different circumstances may require different conclusions.

NEVER ASSUME that because as a leader you are confident with a change, everyone else will be comfortable with it too. Change requires communication. You must sell the change, or chaos will be the result.

NEVER ASSUME change will not be costly. Change is not cheap!

NEVER ASSUME people will take responsibility unless they are given responsibility and the means to measure it.

NEVER ASSUME your expectations will be met unless you let others know what your expectations are.

NEVER ASSUME a standard will be met because a standard was set. It is the leader's job to hold the team accountable.

NEVER ASSUME little details will not make a big difference.

NEVER ASSUME yesterday's accomplishments will assure or guarantee tomorrow's success. The past will not always last.

NEVER ASSUME the strength of an organization will be sustained.

NEVER ASSUME that if you are being successful, you deserve all the credit. A great leader takes the blame and gives away the credit.

NEVER ASSUME that because you are experiencing a degree of success, there is no need to change what you are doing.

NEVER ASSUME what you are doing will get better without evaluating it and enhancing it.

NEVER ASSUME that because something was excellent, it cannot be improved upon. Evaluate everything!

NEVER ASSUME that because something was excellent, it does not need to be eliminated.

NEVER ASSUME that because you are busy, you are being productive. Activity does not equal accomplishment.

NEVER ASSUME that because something is working well in another environment, it will work well in yours.

NEVER ASSUME that because something is not working well in another environment, it will not work well in yours.

NEVER ASSUME the grass is always greener on the other side. You will find out when you get there that it needs cut and fertilized too.

NEVER ASSUME failure is final. Sometimes failure is the best classroom for future success.

NEVER ASSUME your passion cannot turn to passivity. Passion must be stoked.

NEVER ASSUME setbacks are bad. Sometimes you need more time for a better plan.

NEVER ASSUME that when things are bad, they can't get worse.

NEVER ASSUME that because you're prepared and the plan is in place, you will not have to improvise.

NEVER ASSUME that a "little" character flaw cannot be fatal.

NEVER ASSUME that talent qualifies someone to be a team player.

NEVER ASSUME that because someone said they have experience or expertise in an area, he or she can do the job to your level of expectation.

NEVER ASSUME that because you've been the right leader to bring your team to where they are, you are the right leader to take them where they need to be.

NEVER ASSUME humility qualifies someone as a servant leader.

NEVER ASSUME everyone who desires to be a leader deserves to be a leader.

NEVER ASSUME someone who has leadership potential will develop into a leader without being developed by another leader.

NEVER ASSUME your team can repeat your vision unless it is continuously repeated.

NEVER ASSUME you are the only one capable of making the correct decision.

NEVER ASSUME something or someone is great just because someone told you that; check it out for yourself.

NEVER ASSUME your attitude will not affect the attitude of your team and organization. Your attitude will usually set the tone for the team.

NEVER ASSUME a bad attitude cannot be broken, and NEVER ASSUME it will go away without dealing with it today.

NEVER ASSUME that if you ignore it, it will go away.

NEVER ASSUME that if you put it off, it will get easier.

NEVER ASSUME the probability of a problem. Sometimes the littlest things can cause the greatest headaches.

NEVER ASSUME that because many view you as a leadership hero, there are not those who view you as a leadership villain.

NEVER ASSUME that because criticism is being made, a correction must be made. Sometimes your loudest critics will attack you when you are going in the right direction.

NEVER ASSUME all criticism is invalid. Sometimes that information can be invaluable to your future success.

NEVER ASSUME personal growth without a plan for personal growth. Growth is never automatic. Develop an intentional personal growth plan.

NEVER ASSUME you can stay effective and "on the edge" of your career without regular seasons of rest and relaxation. Even God rested on the seventh day.

NEVER ASSUME that because you appreciate your team, they feel appreciated. Take time to prove your appreciation to them.

NEVER ASSUME you must be serious all the time to take your responsibilities seriously. It's okay to laugh, smile, and enjoy your job.

NEVER ASSUME a shortcut will save time. Sometimes the longest way to do something is the shortcut.

NEVER ASSUME there is a sequel to success unless you repeat what it took to get you there.

NEVER ASSUME the highest level of influence only comes from the highest level of leadership.

NEVER ASSUME a proposal is as promising as it has been promoted.

NEVER ASSUME your past automatically prepares you for your future.

NEVER ASSUME experience equals expertise.

NEVER ASSUME good people are not capable of doing bad things.

NEVER ASSUME it's over until it's over!

NEVER ASSUME your idea is the ideal idea. The best leaders benefit from the best ideas because they bring the best people to the table to think innovatively and creatively.

Exceptions to the Rule: The 7 Times It is Safe to Assume:

1. When you have enough evidence or assurance that something is true
2. When you have explored something to the point where you feel completely comfortable
3. When you have communicated your expectations clearly, and those involved clearly understand their role or responsibilities
4. When you don't care the outcome of a matter
5. When you don't have a deadline or something to deliver
6. When you don't mind looking foolish
7. When you don't mind taking a loss or a setback

   ...otherwise, NEVER ASSUME!

"Erroneous assumptions can be disastrous."
   —Peter Drucker

Developing Teams: 4 Types of Teams

1. DESTRUCTIVE teams are harmful, hazardous, and toxic.

   - They are dysfunctional. They cause great damage and bring very little advantage to the organization. They are a liability to longevity.
   - They are disruptive and destructive, full of division and tension.
   - Destructive teams can be very disruptive to the health of an organization.

   Some common traits of destructive teams:
   - Arrogance. When excessive pride resides on a team, there is usually division within the team.
   - Indifference (apathy, don't care)
   - Unhealthy alliances and allegiance
   - Unhealthy conflicts (personal or political conflicts rather than healthy ideological conflicts)
   - Maintenance mindset
   - Lack of trust among team members
   - Lack of accountability
   - Poor results

- Resistance or defiance to a person, process, or plan.
- Incompetence (individual or corporate—poor performance). Always drags a team down.
- Dominance by one or more individuals, including the leader/boss.

Things will not automatically get better; you must address issues and team members and alter some things. You can't keep doing the same thing expecting different results. (This is insanity.)

2. DECENT teams have harmony, but not a lot is happening.
- These are good teams, but they need improvement.
- This is a dangerous type, especially if you've served on a destructive team. You think things are good but know they are not great. And because there is not a lot of conflict on the team, you are content.
- They have talent but need improvement. They are lacking an environment of development.
- The team plays to the level of the individuals' level of talent. These teams often have some solo superstars. They have some great

players on the team. but they don't play together as a team.

- A picture of this might be Peter, who was not mindful of the things of God, but of men. Peter had great potential but was not living up to it.
- You end up content instead of being intent to invent.
- They don't necessarily cause problems but are not high on production.
- There are a lot of good things to say about a decent team: they get along, they don't cause a lot of problems, they are faithful to do their work, and they get things done.
- They are healthy and helpful but are missing a few ingredients that would make their team successful.

3. DEVELOPED teams harness the energy and synergy of the team and can accomplish great things as a group.

- The degree of team greatness is determined by its level of development and investment.
- Great teams have depth because they are fully and faithfully developed. (Both are important.)
- The word "develop" means to bring out the capabilities or possibilities of, to bring to a

more advanced or effective state, to grow or expand.

- These teams and individuals have been coached to the next level.
- They involve a lot of work. They don't evolve or happen on their own. There is no "Big Bang" theory on teams.
- You must maintain them to obtain your desired objectives.

4. DEMORALIZED teams are hampered by a system, structure, or supervisor.

- There has typically been an event or experience that caused the team or individuals on the team to be deflated.
- An example of this would be the disciples after the Crucifixion.
- Notice what Jesus does. He showed up and restored them. (John 21)
- A leader needs to keep a pulse on the health of the team. A demoralized team can jeopardize the organization's mission.
- Developed teams left dormant deteriorate. They must be continually coached.

A Few Final Observations About Developing Teams:

- Teams do not automatically and dramatically improve without intentional investment from leadership.
- Your team will never be ideal until you deal with its problems.
- Continuous improvement requires continuous investment.
- Retention of a developed team requires regular attention to the team. A developed team can deteriorate and be demoralized.
- The senior leader must be the primary facilitator. Team development is one aspect of leadership a senior leader cannot fully delegate.
- You don't have to be an expert to start/try.

"In developing teams, I don't believe in rules. I believe in standards. Rules don't promote teamwork; standards do." —Mike Krzyzewski

Strategies for Setting Boundaries

Henry Cloud said, "Boundaries are made up of two essential things: what you create and what you allow. A boundary is a property line. It defines where your property begins and ends. If you think about your home, on your property, you can define what is going to happen there and what is not."

Boundaries establish the perimeter while providing protection.

Boundaries are the markers we set to help us better manage the property we are responsible for.

Never assume your boundary is abundantly clear. It is dangerous to assume boundary lines are obvious to everyone.

14 Strategies for Setting Boundaries in Your Life:

1. Understand the benefits and benefactors of boundaries.

2. Personalize and prioritize your boundaries to capitalize on them.

3. Publish once you establish your list so that your boundaries are well known.

- I can't expect you to respect my boundaries if you don't know where they are.
- Communicate them properly, clearly, and regularly.
- It is important to:
  - Survey your boundaries.
  - Set your boundaries.
  - Share your boundaries.
  - Stay within the boundaries set.

4. Practice what you preach (what you prioritize).
- "Boundaries need to be communicated first verbally and then with actions." —Henry Cloud
- Boundaries are not beneficial if you continually trespass them.
- Inventory your priority list and then take authority over it.
- Be aware of areas in your life that could impair (disqualify) your leadership.
- Set realistic goals for implementation and improvement.
- Clarify and distinguish what you need, what you want, and what would be nice to have.
- Be persistent and consistent in the implementation.

5. Repeat what you want to reinforce, and review what you enforce.
   - Just because you communicated it does not mean everyone comprehended it.
   - Remind people by repeating what is important to you. (Good news is, eventually they will get it.)

6. Know when and how to say no.
   - Remember that "No" is a complete sentence." — Annie Lamott
   - "The most basic boundary-setting word is 'no.' It lets others know that we exist apart from them and know that we are in control of ourselves." —Dr. Henry Cloud and Dr John Townsend

7. Don't settle for one fence of defense.
   - Set boundaries on all your borders.
   - There are at least 4 borders you need to cover:
     o Professional life
     o Personal life
     o Private life (Character is who you are when no one is looking.)
     o Preferred life

8. Establish your exceptions or exemptions.

9. Learn to filter before you alter your plans.
   - Don't fill or finalize your plans without using the filter
   - Set up some safeguards so you don't get caught.
   - Audit your audibles.

10. Minimize the urge to rationalize or apologize for the boundaries you set.
    - Resist the urge to explain your boundaries or make excuses for having them. That just gives people something to argue with you about.
    - Some suggest you practice your speech in advance.
    - You will encounter people who will encourage you to set boundaries but see themselves as the exception to that boundary.
    - You will have people who are upset by the boundaries you set, especially if it impacts them.
    - Prepare to get pushback when you enforce your boundaries. The pushback is not usually when you set the stake but when you act on it. "The only people who get upset about you setting boundaries are the ones who were benefiting from you having none." — Unknown

- Don't let your pushback set back your boundaries.

11. Practice The Golden Rule. Exemplify your expectations.
    - Do to others as you would have them do to you. (Matthew 7:12)
    - Practice what you preach. People will imitate what you practice.
    - Respect the boundaries other people enforce, even if they don't make sense. The exception to this is if you are the boss, and a boundary impacts a responsibility of the employee.
    - Respect boundaries others have set. Don't call or interrupt your staff on their day off if you want them to respect you on yours.

12. Review and refine your boundaries from time to time.
    - After you define your boundaries, it is smart to revisit them to see if they need to be refined.
    - Ask yourself this question: "How is that working out?" Remember, negative feedback does not necessarily mean your boundary needs to be changed.
    - Bring others into this discussion. Get their input.

13. Approach a coach to help you broach the subject of boundaries.
    - There are 2 ways we could tackle this:
        o I could tell you what you should do, and in the end, you could tell me it will not work for you.
        o I can coach you and ask key questions. You are the expert.

14. Add accountability to your boundaries.
    - In the process of developing boundaries, give someone access to approach you and ask hard questions.
    - Grant this "referee" permission to "throw the flag"—to call a foul or out-of-bounds.
    - Who is your referee to let you know you are out of bounds?
    - Instant replay (Review and evaluate.)

"The only difference between you and someone that you envy is that you settled for less."
— Megan Kelly

"Growth is the great separator between those who succeed and those who do not. When I see a person beginning to separate themselves from the pack, it's almost always due to personal growth." —John C. Maxwell

"Unless you try to do something beyond what you have already mastered, you will never grow." —Ralph Waldo Emerson

A Few Fundamental Truths Regarding Growth:

- Growth is not inevitable.
    o It does not happen automatically or accidentally.
    o Intention + Action = GROWTH
    o Doing nothing does not produce the desired outcome.
    o "Change is inevitable. Growth is optional." —John C. Maxwell

- Your growth is not dependent on the interest of anyone else to increase.
  - It's called a PERSONAL growth plan.
  - While it can be helpful to be in an environment where people want to grow, if you have personal discipline, you can develop a personal growth plan.

- Growth is not gained without individual commitment and sacrifice.
  - I cannot grow you without your personal buy-in.
  - I look to invest my life in people who are hungry, available, faithful, teachable, and leadable.

- Growth is not instantaneous.
  - It does not happen all at once or in a moment.
  - It's not usually quick, but brick by brick.
  - While growth does not happen in a day, it is a daily discipline.
  - "The secret of your success is determined by your daily agenda". —John C. Maxwell
  - Growth is a purposeful, long-term process.
  - "Little by little, a little becomes a lot." —Tanzanian proverb

- Growth should not be isolated to only one area of our life.
  - That is what is so impactful about this idea. If I'm growing a little bit in each of the key areas of my life, I'm still growing.
  - Too often leaders make the mistake of trying to develop and grow only one specific area of their life. The end result of that approach is imbalance.

- Growth is not the result of intermittent effort or action.
  - "Strength and growth come only through continuous effort and struggle."
    —Napoleon Hill
  - "All growth depends upon activity. There is no development physically or intellectually without effort, and effort means work."
    —Calvin Coolidge

- Growth does not happen without a plan that includes intentional ideas which inspire a desired future.
  - Vision is a picture of a preferred future. A personal growth plan is a tool to help you pursue that preferred future.
  - These ideas must be intentional and implemental, and that requires a plan.

- o "I find it fascinating that most people plan their vacations with better care than they plan their lives. Perhaps that is because escape is easier than change." —Jim Rohn

Your GROWTH GOALS should:
- Be specific
- Stretch you (Don't just put down something you are already doing.)
- Be stated simply
- Be sequenced in terms of priority
- Be written down
- Be shared with others for the sake of accountability
- Be studied regularly (reviewed and revised)
  - o Growth cannot be managed unless it is being measured.

A personal growth plan can be divided into 3 buckets:
1. Professional life (work)
2. Personal life (key relationships)
   - Faith
   - Family
   - Friends
3. Private life

Ask yourself this key question: "What can I do in these areas of my life that will facilitate and forward a level of intentional growth?"

Time Management

Your use of time is an alarm that goes off awakening everyone to your true leadership ability. The way you manage time is a good indicator of how you will manage a task.

Theology of Time (Time has spiritual implications.):
- There is a time for everything. (Ecclesiastes 3:1)
- God works on an appointed time frame. (Romans 9:9)
- Time is short. (1 Corinthians 7:29; Revelation 12:12)
- We are to be making the most of/"redeeming" our time. (Ephesians 5:16; Colossians 4:5)

5 Things that Will Not Improve Your Time Management Skills:

1. Excuses
2. Procrastination
3. Blame
4. Desire (Wishing it will get better)
5. Dumping on others (There's a difference between dumping and delegation.)
   - Someone can bail you out of your tight spot, but you will be right back into it unless you learn how to manage your time.

"Everything requires time. It is the only truly universal condition. All work takes place in time and uses up time. Yet most people take for granted this unique, irreplaceable, and necessary resource. Nothing else, perhaps, distinguishes effective executives as much as their tender loving care of time."
—Peter F. Drucker

The value of time is the common denominator of all successful leaders.

Time is the scarcest resource of the manager; if it is not managed, nothing else can be managed.
—Peter Drucker

"Time management is really a misnomer. The challenge is not to manage time but to manage ourselves." —Stephen Covey

The Value of Managing Attention Even More Than Time:
- "Attention is the currency of leadership." —Ronald A. Hiefetz
- "Pay attention to what you are paying attention to so you can be intentional about what you are attending to." —Steve Sartori

21 Time Management Tips:

1. Build quiet time into your schedule for prayer and devotion. You will be amazed at how when you honor God with your time, things work out.

   - It was Martin Luther who once said, "I have got so many things to do today, I will have to spend the first three hours in prayer."
   - This happens to be the most overlooked time management practice. When we are extremely busy, this is usually the first thing we cut out.

   Quiet time is important to time management because:

   - It is through quiet time that we receive strength for the tasks that lie ahead.
   - It is through quiet time that we understand and discern God's will for each day.
   - It is through quiet time that we surrender our will and submit to His. ("Your will be done on earth" —Jesus Christ)
   - It is through quiet time that we present our requests to God. Our requests ought to include God's intervention in our day— helping things to work out.

2. To budget your time more efficiently, take a week and track how you are spending your time.

Write down what a week looks like and where you are spending your time. You cannot improve your time management if you don't know where your time is going.

- If you were having budget problems, the first thing a financial adviser would suggest is that you do a short-term audit of how you are spending your finances so you can see where your money is going.
- "Effective executives do not start with their tasks. They start with their time. And they do not start out with planning. They start by finding out where their time goes. Then they attempt to manage their time and to cut back unproductive demands on their time." —Peter Drucker
- Being busy is not the same as being productive. Activity does not equal productivity.

One of the most valuable things we can do to improve our time management is eliminate some of the things we are doing. Evaluation should lead to elimination of things that are not effective.

- "Identify and eliminate the things that need not be done at all" —Peter Drucker

3. One of the best ways to save time is to take time to determine what your values and priorities are in life.

- As John C. Maxwell says, "It's not a matter of prioritizing your schedule but scheduling your priorities."
- "How different our lives are when we really know what is deeply important to us, and keeping that picture in mind, we manage ourselves each day to be and to do what really matters most." —Stephen Covey
- "Whenever leaders are seduced into investing time in the trivial, they have become disengaged from the essential." —Henry Blackaby

4. Invest adequate time to develop organizational systems that allow you to stay on top of things.
   - When it comes to shuffling papers, forget it, file it, or forward it to someone else.

5. Develop healthy habits and routines.
   - Henry Blackaby said, "Wise leaders use routines to ensure that their priorities are never overlooked."
   - They can save a great deal of time because the planning aspect of routines has already been accomplished.

6. Live each day by a daily planner. Your daily planner can make a yearly difference. Never start your day until you have finished it on paper.

7. Start your day on time. When you start behind, you generally stay behind. When you start the day rushing, you usually end up running behind.

8. Divide your time into smaller, more manageable portions.
   - "Nothing is particularly hard if you divide it into small jobs." —Henry Ford
   - "Start by doing what's necessary, then what's possible, and suddenly you are doing the impossible." —St Francis of Assisi

9. Address and attack your hardest tasks first thing, when your energy level is the greatest.

10. Whenever possible, multitask for greater efficiency.
    - Dr. Richard Swenson says that because our culture is so fascinated with multitasking, we are diminishing the margin in our lives.
    - Be careful with multitasking. Research demonstrates that it is rapid attention switching, leaving behind "attention residue," which takes more time in the end.

11. Be realistic with your planning. Don't set yourself up for discouragement or failure by making your daily list too long. Manage your tasks throughout the week and the month.

Better yet, calendarize as much as possible, being cognizant of Hofstadter's Rule: "Everything takes longer than you think."

12. Make good time choices. Watch out for time wasters.

13. Delegate to others tasks that you don't need to be doing or that they do better than you.

    4 Things You Can Do with a Task:
    - Delete or decline it. (Say no.)
    - Delay it (Schedule it for a later date.)
    - Dedicate your time and energy to it. (Do if it is something only you can and should do.)
    - Delegate it. (to the right person.)

    Brian Tracy warns us to avoid "reverse delegation."

    There is a huge difference between delegating and dumping.

14. Stay in the driver's seat when it comes to your time. If you don't, other people will. (When scheduling meetings with people, say, "I've got 30 minutes" or, "I've got one hour.")

15. Look ahead, think ahead, and plan ahead. Last-minute matters are often time killers.

- Build into your planning time to look far enough ahead so that you are not blind-sided by something urgent.
- This is also where short-term goals and long-term goals are effective in helping us to accomplish more in the future.

16. When it comes to meetings, remember they can be huge time wasters.
    - Set a time.
    - Start on time.
    - Stay on time.
    - Shut down on time. (Schedule another meeting if you must.)

17. Set boundaries with your time.
    - How much time will I spend surfing the internet?
    - How much time will I spend on social media?
    - How much time will I spend writing and responding to emails?
    - How much time will I spend on a project?
    - What is the standard for excellence I desire to achieve?
      - People who have a perfectionistic tendency waste a great deal of time because there is always one more thing they can do to make it better.

18. Build in time for being interrupted and getting caught up. One of the greatest frustrations for task-oriented people is being interrupted when on a roll.

    - Create systems of communication to let team members know when a good or bad time for interruption is (open or closed door, blinds).

19. The best way to be efficient with your time is to equip your team to be efficient with theirs. Teach people you work with time management principles. Teach them to be more efficient with their time, and it will make things easier for you as well. Require your team to use a daily planner.

20. Time out! In sports, clock management can be the difference between winning and losing. The same is true in your job or ministry. Make sure you take time off weekly as well as get away throughout the year.

21. Read and invest as much as you can on time management resources.

    Realize this important truth: you can't implement it all at once. Just take on one new idea at a time and turn it into a habit over the next 21 days.

DIG

REPORTS

Date: Area of responsibility:

D Things I've **DONE** in my leadership role during the past week.
- Give an update on your goals from the previous report.
- List of accomplishments and activities. (Be specific.)
- Things I've checked off my DO LIST

I **INFORMATION** I need to share with other team members.
- What information will other team members need to know from my area of ministry?
- Ideas for improvement or implementation

G **GOALS** for the coming week/month (Be very specific.)
- What are the goals I have in the coming week (before our next report)?
- Focus on looking ahead. What needs to be done?

Any action items:
Prayer requests:
Submitted by:

More Leadership Proverbs

It's valuable to a team when its leaders are vulnerable with its members.

Leadership is developing someone or something to its fullest potential.

Well-being is aligning with God's design in our lives.

Leadership ability without adaptability becomes a liability in any leadership culture.

A good leader exemplifies his own expectations.

Your experience as a leader is usually tied to your expectations as a leader.

Leaders must adopt an adaptable mindset. Those who can't adapt often get slapped.

If you always look at people through the lens of defects and deficits, you will define and defeat them. Look at them with respect and expect to see a different effect. (Pygmalion effect—You get what you expect.)

It's always more impactful to lead with a carrot instead of a club.

Your title does not entitle you to respect.

No response is a NO response. It is always courteous to respond to a request.

When a leader assumes, danger looms.

Duplication is the abdication of innovation. You waste creativity when you just copy and paste.

Some leaders are good at making bad decisions (or bad at making good decisions).

When your leadership or organizational structure restricts leaders from leading, you essentially release them to leaving.

Learn to confirm appointments and affirm improvements as a leader.

Followers are fond of a leader who will respond to any gesture of help or kindness with a quick thank you. Say it and send it. You can't show enough appreciation.

An early lead can be misleading. Don't give up until time's up.

What gets recognized and rewarded gets repeated.

A lot of people are focused on, "What is your VISION for the future?" I think it's just as important to ask, "What are your VALUES for the present?"

Irritation is the initial indication of the potential presence of anger. There is a fine line between being irritated and becoming irate.

Failure to address the stress in your life will ultimately lead you into a state of distress.

It is never an asset when regret becomes your prevailing mindset.

Momentum begins with movement, so get started.

The best time to debate an idea or issue is in the discussion and inception phase, not the departure and implementation phase. After the ship sets sail is not the time to determine its destination.

A negative reaction or response does not always require an alternate route. Sometimes it requires staying the course, regardless of the reaction.

Sometimes people need to be pushed before they will be positive. Change can be initially uncomfortable.

Leaders must be thermostats, not thermometers. Everything rises or falls on leadership.

Leaders will not go on strike just because their followers dislike something.

You can handle anything within reason for a season. Endurance often makes the difference in leadership.

Christian courage is an unconditional confidence in the providence of God.

It's always helpful when a leader is hopeful about the future. Being positive can have a powerful impact on your team and your organization.

Practice does not always make perfect, but it can correct a defect. Practice makes predictable, not perfect. Only perfect practice makes perfect.

Relationship is a powerful portion of leadership. Respect requires relationship.

Frustration can be the foundation for bringing something to fruition.

Beware of an unaware leader; he can cause great despair.

The best of intentions is never a match for the introduction of action. Good intentions create tensions when they are not accompanied by actions. Good intentions do not guarantee a positive impact.

Leaders often distract from the outcome because they are abstract in their expectations.

You don't have to be an expert to be alert to the needs of your people.

The best way to abound in leadership is to make sure you surround yourself with great leaders.

Be careful. Your temperament can be impacted by the treatment you receive. Forgive, and keep short accounts of those who mistreat you. (1 Corinthians 13:5)

Learn to laugh with your staff, not at your staff. A work environment that is fun is more functional that one that is not.

Be wise with your use of humor in the workplace. It can be helpful or harmful.

Great leaders never belittle the little. It's the little foxes that spoil the vine. (Song of Solomon 2:15)

The coarseness of a leader can be a very careless leadership trait.

For vision to be realized, it needs to be visualized and verbalized regularly.

When followers question your leadership, you can either crumble in despair, mumble in frustration, or be humble in character: you decide. (Numbers 12:1-3) Put on Humility. (Colossians 3:12)

The anchor of a leader is tested by whether he weathers the storms or is washed away by them.

The real measure of a leader is weighed through times of adversity, not times of affirmation.

Leaders do not run from conflict; they get involved to resolve it.

We can only advance to the next level of leadership by passing the test of leadership. If we fail the test, we must either repeat the course or drop out. Our goal is not to just pass the test but to make the dean's list. The best leadership lessons come through a storm rather than through a seminar.

In resolving conflict, it's not about who's right but about making things right.

Leadership not only involves rising to the occasion, but sometimes rising above the occasion.

Spirit-led strategic planning is the process of discerning, discovering, and documenting God's direction for your organization. There is a difference between self-guided strategic planning and Spirit-led strategic planning. One is guided by the principles and practices of the world; one is guided by the precepts of the Word of God.

Criticism is the sales tax of success. The greater the success, the greater the tax.

Just because you desire it does not mean you deserve it. Eliminate entitlement thinking. Doing the next hard thing helps stifle entitlement thinking.

A cynical attitude is never a pinnacle accomplishment for a leader.

Raise your expectations and standards.

Your opinion should never take dominion over evidence and facts.

A leader must ensure the durability of his credibility. Credibility adds stability to the leader and the organization.

Develop your leadership team so that every member is empowered to contribute to the solution you need.

Always make it apparent that you are being transparent. Doubt will destroy your leadership credibility.

Don't exaggerate. It will only frustrate your team and deteriorate your own leadership. You don't formulate trust when you exaggerate truth.

Being arrogant will usually end in embarrassment. Pride always goes before a fall. (Proverbs 16:18)

A leader must evidence a balance of confidence in themselves and a dependence on their team.

Leading a group forward does not depend upon seniority or superiority as much as a recognized and respected authority.

The right attitude will give you tremendous latitude in leadership.

We often mistake the outrageous for the courageous.

"Narcissistic" is a terrible characteristic for a leader to possess.

When we think of change, our first thought is usually of the pain, not the gain, associated with the change.

Our readiness to change will ultimately impact our effectiveness in the process of change. People view change as either a threat or an asset.

Some leaders don't initiate change because they are intimidated by change.

Change that is not uncomfortable is usually change that is unprofitable. Leaders must get comfortable with being uncomfortable.

Confidence is never a coincidence.

Worry is a leader's worst friend. Worry never adds anything positive to the end of the story.

"Worry is like a rocking chair. It gives you something to do but never gets you anywhere." —Erma Bombeck

"Worrying is like paying a debt you don't owe." —Mark Twain

"I've had a lot of worries in my life, most of which never happened." —Mark Twain

A smart leader understands that his team does not exist to assist him but the mission of the group.

Leaders understand there is a difference between dangerous and courageous. One is ridiculous; the other is just risky.

A leader needs to predict conflict prior to becoming a problem. It's called intuition.

A counterpunch can be counterproductive in leadership. Sometimes it is best to just turn the other cheek. (Matthew 5:39)

You don't have to worry about having trouble with traffic when you travel the extra mile. (Matthew 5:41)

You cannot be a reformer in leadership if you are stuck as a conformer in the status quo.

You will never advance a change without giving it a chance to work. Change requires resiliency.

In life and leadership, adversity can often be the best university for personal growth.

Effective leaders are outrageously courageous.

Self-discovery is often sabotaged by self-deception.

A wise leader will conceal his aggravation against people and reveal his appreciation for people.

There is a difference between an appointed leader and an anointed leader. The first will be followed out of responsibility; the second will be followed out of respect.

Sometimes a prolonged decision can be just as damaging as a wrong decision.

Building time into your schedule for daily, honest reflection is one of the healthiest ways to gain insight into a necessary course correction.

Debrief your beliefs to achieve greater results. Your current beliefs may be a deterrent to your long-term accomplishments.

Biblical leadership is not just a personal asset, mindset, or even a skillset, but a reset of God's presence and power in and through your life.

One piece of leadership advice every leader should consider before he acts: Don't advance before you get wise advice. (Proverbs 20:18)

Avoiding an unnecessary fight is the right thing to do. (Proverbs 20:3)

A spirit that is suspicious always suspends confidence.

When it comes to well-being, leaders are either thriving, surviving, or need reviving.

Organizations frequently get off track because of a rift within the organization, a drift in the organization's mission, or the failure of the mission to pivot and make a necessary shift to stay on target.

Leaders need to learn how to compete and complete even when things get complicated.

Progress is an excellent way to impress people you report to in leadership.

Persistence can be very persuasive. Don't give up. (Luke 18:1-8)

The tombstone of an ineffective leader reads, "He led alone."

A double standard can cause unnecessary trouble for a leader. (Proverbs 20:10)

Unlock and unleash the cage to engage your team. Value their opinions and listen to their ideas.

It's effective when you find someone who is objective and can bring a different perspective.

Being reliable is a clear, identifiable characteristic of faithful leadership.

Collaboration within your corporation is the key to transformation.

The key to getting started is to stop procrastinating. You can't gain momentum without movement.

If you care about continuous improvement, don't be afraid to seek a critique from time to time.

With God's help and hand, leaders' triumph through trauma.

Leaders focus on mediation during the midst of polarization.

Consistency is the common currency used by successful leaders.

Common sense can be your best offense in moving forward. (Proverbs 21:16)

Outward concern without inward consciousness is outrageously dangerous.

Even when you can't control the outcome, you can still influence the input.

The end often depends on your endurance.
(Matthew 24:13)

The true measure of a leader is how he performs under pressure. (Proverbs 24:10)

The easiest slide from success is to glide in your pride rather than to continuously strive for improvement. (Proverbs 16:18)

Sincerity, charity, and clarity go a long way towards the solidarity of a group.

Leaders who lead alone are prone to failure. You will get along better if you bring others with you.

"If you want to go fast, go alone. If you want to go far, go together." —African proverb

A healthy leadership culture needs to be intentionally cultivated within the organization.

You may be in a position of transition, but don't settle there. Focus on the acquisition of transformation.

Leaders don't give up when they are knocked down. They get up and keep moving forward. Don't bail because of a single fail. Grow and go on.

A slip is not a fall, a fall is not failure, and failure is not fatal.

When asking a question to someone on your team, don't be afraid of silence once the question is posed. Leave it until they perceive it.

Do everything within your power to prevent resentment. Resentment leads to rage and regret. Resolve it before it evolves.

The outcome will often depend on how much time you spend depending on your own insights, or the wisdom and guidance that can only come from the Lord.

Be upfront to confront conflict. Don't wait until it's too late to deal with it.

Leaders take the proper time to properly de-stress and manage moments of distress in their lives.

A pain point should be a checkpoint for change because pain can drain your energy.

Leaders have an obligation to gain enough information to avoid complication. Do your homework. Carefully review a matter before you pursue a solution.

Leaders do not have the right to do what's right in the wrong way just because they are in a position of leadership.

Every leader has a platform for leadership. Aim to outperform your platform.

There is a difference between bold leadership and leaders who are bullies. (Proverbs 28:1). Don't confuse them as you lead your team.

Relationship is the flagship of effective leadership. When you break relationship, you take away something significant from your ability to lead someone.

We are more likely to change when we feel heat, face defeat, or desire to complete something.

"We don't change when we see the light; we change when we feel the heat." —Rick Warren

Don't be afraid to address the mess you face and then move forward.

Humility and honesty are keys to unity on a team. They bring credibility and stability to leadership. (Proverbs 28:2)

Leaders who possess a partiality mentality rather than neutrality mentality are often biased in their opinions. (Proverbs 28:21)

Leaders should remember to vet their thoughts before they vent their thoughts. (Proverbs 29:20)

Never rely on luck to get you unstuck. Get a coach to help you approach your challenge.

It's a highlight for your team when you share the spotlight. Don't steal the show.

Often impactful questions can be sharpened by being shortened. A long question is not usually the best question.

There would be more civility in leadership if there were more humility in leaders.

Leadership requires lots of persistence and resilience through seasons of prolonged resistance.

One of the best things you can do when you get down is to get up again and take another step. (Proverbs 24:16)

Failure to share the spotlight with others will likely impair your leadership.

Taking the time to observe will serve you well in leadership. Preserve making a judgment until you fully observe a situation.

Advanced planning will give you a better chance to succeed. (Proverbs 24:27)

Don't speak anything you don't want repeated.

Arrange your change; don't leave it to chance.

It is truly a revelation for a leader to understand when to pursue the evolution of change and when to pursue the revolution of change.

When you identify your leadership identity, you have a better idea of how God can work through you.

A team is more likely to follow a leader whose voice casts vision, not just commands.

You lose credibility when you break confidentiality. When your team has confidence in your confidentiality, they will trust you with important secrets.

A contradiction in character is a terrible contribution to leadership. Inconsistency should be inconceivable.

Any time your expectation of others exceeds your expectation of yourself, you're in trouble. That's called hypocritical leadership.

Every day you should reflect and record your observations about leadership. Let your experiences educate you.

The absence of trust creates an obstruction in leadership and invites the presence of disunity.

Sometimes you must adjust your approach to accomplish your objective.

Failure to consider a different point of view can seriously skew the outcome.

Tenacity is the capacity to continue when everything is going wrong.

Adversity is the best university for developing leaders.

A leader can calm a qualm easier with a soothing balm than a sounding bomb.

To correct a problem, a leader must first accept the reality he has stepped into. Complaining does nothing towards correcting the problem. Complaining leads to the problem remaining.

Settling disagreements often depends on the contingency of diplomacy. (Romans 12:18)

Don't hesitate to negotiate a deal if what you revise does not compromise your character and integrity.

A positive attitude will set a powerful mood in your organization.

Be careful not to be careless with your personal care. Don't be so focused on others that you forget your own needs. Manage your margin well for your own well-being.

Prolonged conflict will greatly restrict and afflict the energy and synergy of your environment.

Being proficient at being patient is a powerful leadership quality.

"Through patience a ruler can be persuaded, and a gentle tongue can break a bone" (Proverbs 25:15).

It's critical to carve out space in your calendar to cultivate creativity.

Never underestimate the power of understanding when you are undertaking a challenging situation.

Compassion is the composition of empathy, plus sympathy, minus apathy.

Working together requires companionship, compassion, compromise, and composure.

When you react in rage, it never sets the stage for resolving a matter peacefully.

Failure is often the most effective instruction in life and leadership. The pain will help your memory retain the lesson for the rest of your life. The greater the pain, the longer the memory.

You can bet there will be trouble when you set and let [there be] double standards.

The role of a leader is to add value to other leaders, not to validate his own value. Build up others instead of yourself.

It's hard to wholeheartedly follow a leader who has never been tested first and been found faithful.

Whenever you are perplexed by a complex and complicated problem, set aside some time for solitude to find your solution.

The upside of going through a downward trend is that it will force you to reflect, reimagine, and revamp your current reality.

A season of adversity will often advance your resilience more than a period of prosperity.

The principles of leadership are transferable. If you give yourself to the study of leadership, no matter where you land as a leader, you will be able to lead effectively and efficiently because you have proven yourself teachable.

When your team is all in, you usually have a better outcome.

The ability to provide stability is a powerful
    leadership quality.

Great leaders are first great followers. Following is
just as important as leading. It is through
following other leaders that we learn:

- Humility
- Submission to authority. You are not fully
  prepared to give orders until you are able to
  take orders.
- How to lead. It is on-the-job training. We learn
  what to do and what not to do.
- Another perspective. There is always another
  side of leadership.
- Valuable insight from not being in the
  spotlight.
- How to be a team player/work together as a
  team.

Leaders who hold onto resentment are never able
    to lead out of a place of true contentment.

Effective leaders don't spend their time comparing
    themselves to other leaders; they spend their
    time preparing themselves to be better leaders.

You amplify your leadership when you apply
    yourself to learning.

The relentless pursuit of preparation is what leads to excellence.

It's too late to get ready when reality arrives. Have an arrow ready for any possible scenario.

Great leaders give ample example of their expectations.

Create movement toward improvement, and you will encounter momentum along the way.

It's the little details that make a big difference in leadership.

Make sure there is a spirit of cooperation within your corporation, or there will be a lot of complication.

Leaders are willing to address any selfish success within their business.

Read and feed your mind with great books that stretch you, strengthen you, and are strategic for your role in leadership.

A leader who leads on emotion without reason can create a lot of commotion. They need to keep their poise even when there is a lot of noise.

Keep in mind that your way is not always the best way. Keep an open mind to other ideas and opinions to see if there might be another way that is a better way.

Leadership is the ability to project and protect stability in seasons of vulnerability.

Don't let your confidence be interpreted as arrogance.

Collect your thoughts and connect your thoughts before you try to communicate your thoughts.

Your resilience either suffers or is sufficient, depending on your relationships.

Beware of the entourage of people who like to sabotage the vision through division.

As a leader, be alert to those in the group who prefer to revert to the past instead of the future.

It's not unusual to be annoyed by someone who is employed in your organization. What is uncommon is the ability to work together through issues and toward a common objective.

Sincerity can bring strong clarity to leadership and life.

You make better decisions by bringing others along with you than by making decisions alone.

A leader should not disgrace himself when he disagrees with someone else. You don't have to be demeaning while you are disagreeing.

Give your team good options instead of just good opinions.

Any time you build the vision on a personality, you limit the long-term possibility of the organization.

Failure can either be fruitful or frustrating, depending on what you learn from it.

Make sure you measure your success with the right metric system.

The degree to which your team can disagree in a healthy manner will decree the well-being of your organization.

Consistency is a proficiency that all leaders should learn to master and maintain.

Your team should complete one another, not compete against one another. You get further faster when you work together.

Your habits will either exhibit or prohibit your future success.

Practice produces confidence.

Awkward moments can create awakening movements.

Pause to clarify the because.

What you see as improbable seems impossible. Be positive and impact the probability.

Pushback is a common comeback from those who want to go back to what used to be.

It takes more than just good luck to get unstuck.

Your ability to review the past is the best opportunity to preview the possibility of the future.

Expanding your view of what's possible is the first step in experiencing a new reality.

Remind yourself from time to time that a closed mind will blind you to open opportunities.

Develop a contingency plan in case of emergency.

Confidence is the evidence and assurance of preparation.

Contemplate your next step before you complicate your next stage.

Never compromise a promise. Don't worm or wiggle away from your word.

Prepare to be fair in all your leadership dealings. Favoritism encourages team schism.

Hurtful comments are never helpful in debating decisions. Remind your team to be kind in conversations and in reaching conclusions.

Capitalize on what you prioritize.

Breaking confidential information creates consequential problems.

The end can justify the means if necessary adjustments are not unjust. Sometimes making an adaptation will give you an advantage.

An atmosphere where complaining is common will have a constraining effect on individual attitudes.

Staying on the moral high ground is impossible if you're playing in the mud.

Your thoughts become your plots, so be careful in what you consider. (Proverbs 23:7)

A differing opinion doesn't have to be divisive. You don't have to be aggressive in your disagreement. Agree to disagree.

Choose your responses wisely. They have the power to enlighten or frighten your team. How you express your thoughts has the potential to distress or suppress the conversation.

Live well, listen well, lead well, and leave well.

True leadership gets revealed when things begin to unravel. True leaders are often revealed on the battlefield.

Lead well. Most healthcare professionals are trained in a trust-and-verify method of leadership rather than a clarify-and-trust approach to leadership.

A mediocrity mentality will never improve the vitality of the organization. "Good enough" is never a great goal.

Leaders often solicit input from team members because they are more interested in affirmation than action steps. Don't ask them questions unless you are willing to act on their potential suggestions.

Innocent intentions can still cause a serious incident.

When things have the appearance of being wrong, they create interference with things going right. (1 Thessalonians 5:22)

A gentle spirit can be an instrumental strength in leadership. Meekness is not weakness.

It's wise for a leader to consult and consider the opinion of others, but when he can't reach consensus, the leader must make the best conscientious decision possible based on all the information available.

Leaders who simplify and identify next steps to complex problems move organizations to completion of the challenges they face.

Sincerity, humility, and unity are a necessity when building a community in leadership. Any ascent into leadership will be difficult if these qualities are absent.

Disguising our insecurities instead of discussing them can result in compromising trust instead of capitalizing on it. Being vulnerable can be a valuable leadership trait.

Prioritize to capitalize your task list. Determine and differentiate if tasks are:

- Immediate (Need to be done NOW)
- Important (Need to be done SOON)
- Impending (Need to be done SOMETIME)

"The mark of a great man is one who knows when to set aside the important things in order to accomplish the vital ones." —Brandon Sanderson

The decision is obvious when it's unanimous, but it can be precarious when the group is contentious about moving forward.

Effective leaders have learned to diffuse the excuses in their life. They execute their excuses.

Instability impairs your capability to serve to your full capacity.

A leader can be conflicted and still be convinced he is moving in the right direction.

A wise leader will awaken when he is mistaken and make some adjustments.

The use of humor in leadership can be helpful, harmful, or hurtful, depending on the intent of the insult. People are rarely resentful when the person making fun is the object of the humor.

When leaders antagonize, they ostracize their team.

You must acquire wisdom to be considered a winsome leader. (Proverbs 4:7)

Bad habits of individual team members tend to inhabit and impact the whole team.

Leaders who regularly read will breed insight into their path.

Opposing opinions have the potential to sharpen your operation.

A little audacity and some tenacity can greatly improve your capacity to persevere.

A leader with respect can be direct and expect the same from their team.

A calm leader decreases the likelihood of explosions even when there is an increase in emotions.

Retrain your brain to complain less and compliment more.

As a leader, don't expect to be an expert in everything. Gather around you people who bring expertise in areas where you are inadequate.

The disbursement of discernment is urgent in leadership.

An unregulated and unguarded virtue can be overthrown by a vice.

Experience can give you a great education if there is demonstration of lessons learned.

As a leader, don't be afraid to disclose seasons of discouragement.

It is an important leadership priority to bring order to your organization.

Leaders are diligent and deliberate to deliberate a matter fully.

You can't continue to hear all day long what's wrong and stay strong without keeping things in perspective.

It's easier to flourish once you have obtained favor.

The impending can be impeding your well-being. The weight of what's coming can be overwhelming.

You need to perceive what's wrong before you can achieve what is right for your organization.

A single interruption can cause a serious disruption to your day.

As a leader, don't abdicate your responsibility to advocate for your team.

It is important for a leader to temper his temper. A hot temper is not a good leadership quality.

It is necessary for a leader to pay attention to areas of tension on his team. Don't ignore the sore spots.

Being under pressure is never a pleasure, but a leader must press on anyway.

Anytime a leader is open to new ideas, new opportunities open.

Remember that new opportunities often create new opposition. Be aware and on guard.

Beware of an unaware leader. Serving with them can be a nightmare.

When you betray trust, you delay advancement and achievement.

It's imperative for a leader to articulate and advocate for any calculated risk in advance of the mission.

The more connected you are when you face the unexpected, the less affected you will be by the unpredictable.

A leader must be able to break out from consequences of burnout, so he doesn't strike out
while he is at the plate.

Respect is a critical aspect of leadership. Protect it
or be wrecked without it. Disrespect will always
have a direct effect in your organization.

It is essential for a leader to have some
providential input to reach his full potential.

The translation of your hesitation to your team is
that you are reluctant—and possibly resistant—
to the idea. Be transparent with your thoughts,
so they don't have to assume.

Your limitations can be a liability without the
versatility of a well-balanced and diverse team.

It's always good for a leader to give a little
exhortation with some explanation of
expectation to avoid the potential of
procrastination.

Give attention to any tension, dissention, or
contention within your team.

Your reactions and responses will determine if people feel reproach or the freedom to approach you.

Be careful not to push back or kick back when your people give you honest feedback.

Hurry feeds worry into your life. Slow down; it will help you settle down.

Consensus is a tremendous form of leadership, except when you are leading through a crisis. In those moments, it will take a singular leadership voice to establish direction and momentum.

Don't let your leadership be ambushed by your ambition.

Slow down, and know how to say no appropriately and effectively.

The time it takes to properly vet someone or something will easily offset the proportionate regret that will surely come if you skip this step.

Three things that can greatly impact your next dilemma: good coaching, wise counsel, and strong conviction. Be cautious whenever one of these is lacking.

It's not only incredibly wrong, but you lose credibility whenever you take credit you don't deserve. Edit the credit and pass it on to the proper person.

The more choices you present, the more likely you are to prevent people from making a good decision. Fewer options enable earlier adoption of an action.

"Can I, do it?" is different than, "Should I do it?" You need to know the difference so you can go the distance.

The amount of rest you get determines the amount of zest you give.

Don't get pressed into saying yes to a request without considering alignment (Does this align with my goals and responsibility?) and confinement (How much will it limit me in my other responsibilities?).

Discontinue the daily practice of discouragement. Everyone gets enough of it. Try engaging each day in encouragement.

Be careful not to confuse what is critical with what is trivial.

It's a shame when leaders resort to blame to cover the results of their own responsibilities. It becomes a blemish on their record.

It's usually a good idea to ask those involved or impacted before you act on impulse.

Leadership sometimes requires speaking up and other times, keeping your mouth shut. (Proverbs 21:23). The right response at the right time will produce the right results.

Your leadership can be fatally flawed without a healthy dose of reality.

Don't let the feeling of rejection become an infection in your determination. Keep pressing on.

Complacency is the currency of the comfortable and content. (Proverbs 1:23)

Visionary leaders can proclaim their goals without knowing how they will obtain them.

Remind yourself that you don't have to be defined by your defeat. Pick up and press on.

Sometimes the only solution to improve the situation is to remove and replace the leader.

Hiring and firing can be a tiring process. Take your time and get it right.

Retribution rarely results in resolution, restitution, or restoration.

As a leader, pay attention to the warning signs of weariness.

A measured approach to leadership is a treasured coach in leadership. Be ready to stay steady for the well-being of your team.

A positive skill set without a proper mindset is not an asset in the long run; it's an upset waiting to happen.

Don't reply on the fly. Wait before you write and reply.

Don't let the battle rattle you. (Exodus 14:14)

Coaching Proverbs

Invite the Holy Spirit to ignite the process. Take a moment to pray and ask the Spirit to lead your conversation.

Make it your intention to keep the attention on the person being coached, not their problem or your need to solve the issue.

A proper agreement with the person being coached is necessary for achievement in the coaching process.

As a coach, it's not your job to convince, convict, or convert the person's thinking but to convey genuine interest and to stay in the conversation.

As the person being coached is beginning to identify issues or information, make sure THEY understand what they're needing as you clarify your understanding of that need.

You don't have to be an expert coach to exert effective coaching principles.

A good coach will stay conscious of the person and curious regarding the conversation.

The cure is connected to the curious. It's advantageous to stay curious.

Never assume that your interpretation of what is being said is what was intended. Keep digging deeper. Clarity is the key to discovery.

Coaches don't draw conclusions; they help make connections through their questions.

Ask people questions that will help them stop and reflect before they respond.

You make a statement to the people you are with when you stay in the moment. When you are "all there," they know you care.

The cues and clues given by the person being coached will provide cues and clues to the coach. Your questions should go with the flow of the conversation.

Be careful not to talk too much as you walk through a coaching conversation.

A fully present coach is pleasant in the eyes and ears of a person being coached.

Think twice before you give advice, and always seek permission of the person being coached.

Coaching is about empowering the person being coached, not about overpowering the conversation.

When coaching, disallow your instinct to repeat what's just been said.

Be careful not to interrupt silence. Have patience whenever there is silence.

Keep your questions concise and precise. Ask them one at a time.

Scrap the recap from the previous session unless the person being coached wants to rewind, review, or report.

Heighten your ability to listen carefully and skillfully.

The best way to make good progress in a coaching conversation is to proceed with the process. Have faith in the process.

Coaching is about facilitating people, helping to empower them in addressing their specific goals and challenges.

Coaching should mostly be a monologue from the person being coached with a little epilogue from the person coaching.

Change your mindset. Don't expect to be the expert when coaching. The person being coached is the expert.

It is important for the coach to explain that he or she should not be expected to be the expert in the conversation; the person being coached is.

Don't interrupt when a client is speaking or interpret what they are saying. When they are finished speaking, continue to ask interesting questions that will help them gain insight from the conversation.

Coaching is not about asking questions; it's about promoting discoveries and acting. You can be full of questions and come up empty on coaching. Ask questions that bring insight, not information.

The difference between mentoring and coaching is that mentors instruct and coaches inquire.

Closed questions close conversations. Open questions open new avenues of exploration.

Absolve yourself of the need to solve their problem. Just because you are involved in the discussion does not mean you are responsible to solve the situation.

You can sharpen your questions by shortening them.

Your attention as a coach throughout the conversation should always be on the person being coached.

Curiosity is a great commodity in coaching. Stay curious in the conversation. Explore thoroughly. Let the person being coached decide when to move on.

Keep the conversation moving forward toward their intended outcome.

Awaken awareness through asking awesome questions.

Continuously move to identify and address any coaching barriers that will help you improve your coaching skills.

The value of a coaching conversation is lowered if it never moves forward. However, there is a powerful moment of discovery before movement and momentum.

Evaluation of each coaching conversation is the key to the elevation of your coaching skills. What went well? What can be improved?

You don't have to be creative to be effective in coaching. Keep your attention on what is being said instead of how you are going to reply.

Even though it's unnatural to be neutral in a conversation, your best option in coaching is to share your opinion sparingly and only with permission.

Always ask permission before you make a recommendation.

Being direct can have a great effect on the conversation.

Let your client give attention to action steps at the end of your conversation.

Coaches don't preside over a client conversation; they come alongside to assist, not insist, with direction.

The coach is not a therapist, but an analyst picking up clues and cues from the conversation. Noticing is a very important tool in coaching.

As a coaching practitioner, practice is the most practical way to improve.

Lean in, listen carefully. Learn more by creatively asking careful questions, then leverage those insights.

Coaching isn't about giving free advice; it's about helping the person being coached find freedom by advancing towards their desired goal.

Questions don't have to be clever, creative, or cute; they only need to be simple and open.

Establishing a clear outcome in your opening agreement will help you overcome any temptation for distraction in the conversation.

Coach your client towards action, not distraction.

If you don't interrupt a pause, it can cause greater awareness and lead to deeper discovery.

Relax when you are coaching and focus on more than just the facts of the conversation.

Let your first question sink in before you link another one. When you stack your questions, they lack impact.

Prayer is a great way to prepare for a coaching conversation. Ask the Lord to guide the direction and decisions that will result from the conversation.

Autonomy is never automatic without autofocus. Autonomy requires intentionality and impartiality through the entire session.

The person being coached is responsible for the selection and direction of the coaching conversation.

Coaching guidelines are designed to be guardrails, not handrails.

Learn how to get more mileage out of metaphors that transpire through the conversation.

Setting a solid agreement with the person being coached is a key to achievement in a valid coaching conversation.

Check in with your client mid-session to check out whether the conversation is on track with the client's goals. Adjust and adapt, if necessary.

Regularly review—and, if necessary, revise—coaching goals if the client desires to go in a different direction.

It's wise to let the client summarize before you finalize the session.

As a coach, serve your client well; they deserve it.

The way you react to your client will have a great impact on the positive or negative outcome.

Action or a change in mindset is a giant step in the right direction.

Perfection is not the goal of a great coaching conversation. The goal is completion of the agreement.

As you unpack the discussion, make sure you stay on track with the direction the client set.

Create space at the end of the coaching session to evaluate the success of the conversation. Do an autopsy of the autonomy of your session.

As you coach, keep this question in mind: If I speak, will it evoke awareness?

Listen carefully to your client; luck will not get them unstuck.

Employ empathy carefully through your coaching conversation.

Have an agreed-upon expectation with your client, then proceed. It's difficult to exceed expectations if you impede the process.

A coach should acquire the desire of the client for the conversation and abandon his own agenda.

Align your curiosity when your client defines his focus for the conversation.

Learn to challenge the person being coached without compromising the coaching process.

Don't give dictation with your observation. Take notice without giving notice.

A great coaching conversation should establish agreement at the beginning and include assessment at the end.

Your coaching will be more effective when you maintain an impartial perspective.

Don't forget that landing the coaching conversation is just as important as leading the conversation.

You can only coach someone who is capable of changing and willing to change.

Coaching is about moving the client forward while the coach is about improving himself.

"Mentors pour in while coaches pull out."
—Tim Roehl

FORWARD COACHING MODEL
to Move a Conversation Forward

As you begin, pray. Ask the Holy Spirit to guide your conversation. (James 1:5)

F   Where do you want to _F_OCUS our coaching conversation? (topic)

O   What is the _O_UTCOME you desire at the end of our conversation?

R   _R_EVIEW your understanding of the focus and outcome. (coach)

W   Identify _W_HAT is standing in the _W_AY? (List any interference.)

A   _A_CTIVATE deeper awareness by asking insightful questions.

R   How will you _R_ESPOND because of this coaching conversation? (What action steps will you take?)

D   _D_ELIVER any direct communication or encouragement.

TRUST THE PROCESS.

Great Leadership Quotes

"Change that is imposed is often change that is opposed." —Steve Sartori

"All disappointment is the result of unmet expectations." —Jimmy Brumbaugh

"Mix idealism with realism and add hard work. This will often bring much more than you could ever hope for." —John Wooden

"A leader must be calm in crisis and resilient in disappointment." —J. Oswald Sanders

"Planning without action is futile; action without planning is fatal." —unknown

"Leadership is the art of disappointing people at a rate they can withstand." —John Ortberg

"A pivot is a change of strategy without a change of vision." —Todd Bolsinger

"Stubbornness is a virtue if you are right." —Tony Dungy

"Success is knowing your purpose in life, growing to reach your maximum potential, and sowing seeds that benefit others." —John C. Maxwell

"The true mark of a Christian leader is trying to build up other people. Raise up other leaders!" —Charles Colson

"Discipline yourself and others won't need to." —John Wooden

"Replace 'how' with 'wow' to build on great ideas. Instead of asking, 'How in the world do you think we can do that?' say, 'Wow, what a great concept!'" —Andy Stanley

"Say 'wow' before 'whoa,' and 'wow' before 'how.'" —Andy Stanley

"Trust is gained like a thermostat and lost like a light switch." —Tod Bolsinger

"One of the best strategies we could find to actually identify future leaders is for me not be in the room" —Danielle Strickland

"You can't wonder and discover when you're in a hurry." —Carey Nieuwhof

"Performance equals potential minus interference." —Timothy Gallwey

"All the competency in the world can't compensate for your lack of character. Ultimately, your character is your lid." —Carey Nieuwhof

"The three Ps of success: passion, persistence, and patience." —Doug Bronson

"Being challenged in life is inevitable; being defeated is optional." —Roger Crawford

"Don't measure yourself by what you have accomplished but by what you should have accomplished with your ability." —John Wooden

"Direction, not intention determines your destination." —Andy Stanley

"Decisions, not desires, determine a man's destiny." —Yang Chen

"What differentiates uncommon leaders is the ability to read a situation before they lead a situation." —Tim Elmore.

There's a passage in Ernest Hemingway's novel, The Sun Also Rises, in which a character named Mike is asked how he went bankrupt: "Two ways," he answers. "Gradually, then suddenly."

"Our greatest fear should not be of failure but of succeeding at things in life that don't really matter." —Francis Chan

"Not everything that is faced can be changed, but nothing can be changed until it is faced." —James Baldwin

"Not everything that can be counted counts. Not everything that counts can be counted." —William Bruce Cameron

"Not everything that can be measured matters, and not everything that matters can be measured." —Albert Einstein

"Nobody can go back and start a new beginning, but anyone can start today and make a new ending." —Maria Robinson

"I can give you a six-word formula for success: Think things through then follow through." —Edward Rickenbacker

"The ultimate measure of a man is not where he stands in moments of comfort but where he stands at times of challenge and controversy." —Martin Luther King, Jr.

"Trust is vital for change leadership. Without trust, there is no travel. When trust is lost, the journey is over." —Tod Bolsinger

"If God is your partner, make your plans BIG!" —D.L. Moody

"Average leaders raise the bar on themselves; good leaders raise the bar for others; great leaders inspire others to raise their own bar." —Orrin Woodward

"The ability to see the good in others and the bad in ourselves is perfect vision." —John Wooden

"The pessimist sees difficulty in every opportunity. The optimist sees opportunity in every difficulty." —J. Oswald Sanders

"The person who sees the difficulties so clearly that he does not discern the possibilities cannot inspire a vision in others." —J. Oswald Sanders

"Often the crowd does not recognize a leader until he has gone, and then they build a monument for him with the stones they threw at him in life." —J. Oswald Sanders

"No leader lives a day without criticism, and humility will never be more on trial than when criticism comes." —J. Oswald Sanders

"Wherever you are, be all there." —Jim Elliot

"Be where your feet are." —Scott O'Neill

"Continuous effort, not strength or intelligence, is the key to unlocking our potential." —Winston Churchill

"Live to the hilt every situation you believe to be the will of God." —Jim Elliot

"We are all faced with a series of great opportunities brilliantly disguised as impossible situations." —Chuck Swindoll

"The working definition of leadership: energizing a community of people toward their own transformation in order to accomplish a shared mission in the face of a changing world." —Tod Bolsinger

"Your irresponsibility eventually becomes someone else's responsibility." —Andy Stanley

"If you listen longer than most people listen, you'll hear things most people never hear." —Carey Nieuwhof

"A great leader's courage to fulfill his vision comes from passion, not position." —John C. Maxwell

"Effective leadership is putting first things first. Effective management is discipline, carrying it out." —Stephen Covey

"A mistake is valuable if you do four things with it: recognize it, admit it, learn from it, forget it." —John Wooden

"We don't learn from experience; we learn by reflecting on experience." —Tod Bolsinger

"The authority by which the Christian leader leads is not power but love, not force but example, not coercion but reasoned persuasion. Leaders have power, but power is safe only in the hands of those who humble themselves to serve." —John Stott

"Don't just delegate tasks to the next generation. If you delegate tasks, you create followers. Instead, delegate authority to create leaders." —Craig Groeschel

"There are two ways to set expectation: get this done now or get this done and here is how." —unknown

"Start by doing what's necessary; then do what's possible; and suddenly you are doing the impossible." —Francis of Assisi

"Stop doing what is easy. Start doing what is right." —Roy Bennett

"The right thing to do is usually the hardest thing to do." —Dr. Bruce Jung

"There is nothing stronger than gentleness." —John Wooden

"If your character is not strengthening, your future is weakening." —Craig Groeschel

"Hope is not a good strategy." —Rick Page

"Hope is not a strategy. Luck is not a factor. Fear is not an option." —James Cameron

"The problem with 'getting even' is it makes you 'even' with someone you don't even like." —Andy Stanley

"Don't mistake activity with achievement." —John Wooden

"People would rather follow a leader that is real than one that is always right." —Craig Groeschel

"To develop resilience in the face of resistance, leaders must stay calm, stay connected, and stay the course." —Richard Blackburn.

"Courage is not simply one of the virtues, but the form of every virtue at the testing point." —C. S. Lewis

"A sense of humor is part of the art of leadership, of getting along people, of getting things done." —Dwight D. Eisenhower

"The solution to an overly busy life is not more time. It's to slow down and simplify our lives around what really matters." —John Mark Comer

"To add value to others, one must first value others." —John C. Maxwell

"Everyone multi-tasks; no one multi-focuses." —David Cooke

"Never forget that only dead fish swim with the stream." —Malcolm Muggeridge

"No one will be remembered for what they just planned to do." —Bob Goff

"I don't want to be successful; I want to be useful." —John MacArthur

"Good outcomes do not lead to excellence; excellence leads to good outcomes. Excellence is not about winning; it's about producing the best result we are capable of achieving." —Richard Stearns

"Delegation is not abdication." —Dan Grider

"The first job of leadership is to love people. Leadership without love is manipulation."
—Rick Warren

"Great leaders have a heart for people. They take time for people. They view people as the bottom line, not as a tool to get to the bottom line."
—Pat Williams

"If I asked customers what they wanted, they would have told me, 'A faster horse!' People don't know what they want until you show it to them." —Henry Ford

"The capacity to learn is a gift. The ability to learn is a skill. The willingness to learn is a choice." —Brian Herbert

"I often say, 'This is what I know today, but I know there's more to know.'" —Tim Elmore

"...what you give your attention to is the person you become. Put another way: the mind is the portal to the soul, and what you fill your mind with will shape the trajectory of your character. In the end, your life is no more than the sum of what you gave your attention to." —John Mark Comer

"You've got to know what makes people tick and what ticks them off." —Steve Sartori

"A person must be big enough to admit their mistakes, smart enough to profit from them, and strong enough to correct them." —John C. Maxwell

"You don't have to be great to get started, but you have to get started to be great." —Les Brown

"If you want it to stay, give it away." —JC Doornick

"Grow through what you go through." —unknown

"Your greatest strength will become your greatest struggle when you take it too far." —David Stevens

"Leadership is creating engagement in what matters most." —Marcus Warner

"Leadership is not where we are taking people, but how we are shaping people." —Erwin McManus

"Leadership is not how do I get people to do what I want them to do, but how do I help them become who they are designed to become." —Erwin McManus

"Motivation is all about emotion." —Marcus Warner

"Don't let the moment you're in mess up the mission you're on." —Jeff Hummel

My Personal Leadership Lists

5 Things that Drive Me Crazy:

1. When people are UN-ORGANIZED
2. When people are UN-PREPARED
3. When people are UN-MOTIVATED (don't take initiative)
4. When people are INCONSISTENT
5. When people leave UN-FINISHED tasks

6 Leadership CAPs (Lids):

1. Capability
2. Capacity (bandwidth)
3. Capital (change in your pocket)
4. Capitalizing on opportunity
5. Capture (the ability to get things done)
6. Captain (to lead)

3 Placement Problems:

1. Placing people into positions of leadership who are not leaders
2. Placing people into positions of service who are not trained
3. Placing people into positions of leadership and service who are not ready. They may be the right people but are not ready to serve.

11 Essential Leadership "Abilities":

1. Flexibility
2. Credibility
3. Stability
4. Sensibility
5. Responsibility
6. Dependability
7. Durability
8. Possibility (thinking)
9. Likeability
10. Availability
11. Accountability

When you are uncertain of your next step, STOP!

<u>S</u>—Survey the situation.
<u>T</u>—Take time to think through your options.
<u>O</u>—Obtain wise counsel.
<u>P</u>—Prioritize then organize a plan to proceed.

4 Necessary Ingredients for Self-leadership to be Successful:

1. Self-awareness (You've got to know yourself.)
2. Self-examination (You've got to look within yourself.)
3. Self-defense (You've got to protect yourself.)
4. Self-control (You have to say no to yourself.)

7 Safeguards Before You Say Yes:

1. Establish a waiting period before responding.
2. Run each opportunity by a loved one. Is he/she okay if you say yes?
3. Examine the actual time commitment that will be expended if you say yes.
4. Consider your capacity. Even if you want to say yes, do you have the time and energy?
5. Ask yourself what you will have to say no to if you say yes to this opportunity. What will suffer if you say yes?
6. Consider the rubric of your priorities, purpose, and passions. How does this fit into your overall mission?
7. Consider your true feelings and desires. Would you be relieved if you refused this opportunity?

Leaders need to THINK: (Proverbs 29:20)

- T—Turn to God for wisdom first. (James 1:5)
- H—Hold off making any judgments until all relevant information is gathered.
- I—Inquire to gain insight and input from trusted advisors.
- N—Navigate an appropriate course of action.
- K—Keep calm, and confidently communicate clearly and consistently.

8 Keys to Succeeding at "Whatever You Do"
(John 2:1-5):

Success is the succession of obedience. Whatever
you do:

1. Commit it to the LORD. (Proverbs 16:3; Psalm 37:5)
2. Do it all for the glory of God. (1 Corinthians 10:31)
3. Do it in Jesus' name. (Colossians 3:17)
4. Work at it with all your heart. (Colossians 3:23)
5. Do it well. (Ecclesiastes 9:10)
6. Remember that you will give an account for how
   you do it. (Romans 14:12; James 2:12)
7. Do it according to the Word of God. (Joshua 1:8)
8. Do it faithfully. (3 John 1:5-7)

When it comes to making things better, there are 3
kinds of people:

1. Those who believe they would be better off
   where they used to be. They have rearview
   mirror vision. They are looking backward, not
   forward. (Numbers 14:3; Ecclesiastes 9:10)

2. Those who believe they are better off where
   things are currently. They don't want to make
   any changes. They like things just the way they
   are. They resist change.

3. Those who believe things could be better off if
   they would explore the potential of new
   possibilities. They are inspired by improvement.

10 Requirements for Biblical Leadership:

When we look at requirements for biblical leadership, we usually consult passages like 1 Timothy 3:1-10 and Titus 1:5-9, but there is also an interesting list the disciples used to recruit leaders. They required:

1. Personal experience with the risen Jesus (Acts 1:21-22)
2. A heart right with God (Acts 1:24, 8:21)
3. Good reputation (Acts 6:3; 1 Timothy 3:7)
4. Full of the Holy Spirit (Acts 6:3)
5. Full of wisdom (Acts 6:3, 10)
6. Full of grace (Acts 6:8)
7. Full of power (Acts 6:8)
8. Basic leadership qualities (Acts 6:3)
9. Full of faith (Acts 6:5,8)
10. Humble (Acts 6:2)

10 Ways Leaders Overcome Challenges:

1. Inspiration and motivation
2. Education
3. Expectations (Set what you expect.)
4. Direction
5. Communication
6. Organization
7. Delegation
8. Participation (the whole team's input and ideas)
9. Confrontation
   - Avoidance is never acceptable.
   - Challenge your challenges.
10. Perspiration (Old-fashioned hard work)

5 Common Leadership Mentalities:

1. They don't think or act when facing a challenge. (They ignore and avoid it.)
2. They act but don't think. (They react and overreact.)
3. They think without acting. (They overthink.)
4. They think and act without consulting key players. (They don't seek additional wisdom.)
5. They think and act appropriately.

11 Things Great Leaders Frequently Say to Their Team:

1. Great job!
2. Thank you for _____ (Be specific when filling in the blank.)
3. I appreciate you. (Give the reason why.)
4. I believe in you.
5. We are better because of you.
6. What do you think? (What is your opinion?)
7. Great idea! (That statement increases great ideas because what gets recognized gets repeated.)
8. WOW! (not how)
9. How can I help you? (or what do you need from me?)
10. That is helpful.
11. I've got your back.

6 Categories of Confidence:

1. No confidence
   - Usually the result of a bad experience.
   - If people following you have no confidence in your leadership, you are not leading, just lingering.

2. Lack of confidence
   - "Confidence is contagious, and so is lack of confidence." —Vince Lombardi
   - "Lack of confidence is a dimmer switch on competence." —Chad Hall

3. Self-confidence

4. Over-confidence
   - Pride goes before a fall. (Proverbs 16:18)
   - Over-confidence comes across as arrogance.
   - Great leaders are confident without being cocky.

5. Lost confidence
   - Confidence is often depleted through defeat and difficulty.

6. God-confident (1 Corinthians 10:12)

12 Things Jesus Taught His 12 Disciples About Real Authority (Matthew 23:1-12):

1. Real authority is not about the position you hold or the place where you sit or serve. (vs. 2, 6)
2. Real authority does not undercut or undermine the authority of others. (vs. 3a)
3. Real authority leads by example, not just by expectation. (vs. 3b)
4. Real authority will help bear heavy burdens, not just bind them. (vs. 4)
5. Real authority will not ask someone to do something they are not willing to do themselves. (vs. 4b)
6. Real authority is unleashed through service, not for show. (vs. 5)
7. Real authority exemplifies humility over honor. (vs. 6)
8. Real authority is not out to make a name or fame for itself. (vs. 7)
9. Real authority lives among, not above, others. (vs. 8)
10. Real authority is given from above (Heaven). (vs. 9-10; Romans 13:1)
11. Real authority does not exist to exalt itself. (vs. 12)
12. Real authority is never political or hypocritical. (vs. 13ff)

Understanding real authority should be a priority of a leader. You can't utilize it if you don't understand it.

4 Buckets Decisions Fall Into:

1. SMART DECISIONS
   - These are wise decisions. Things worked out great.
   - If I had to do it all over again, I would do the same thing.

2. SECOND-GUESSED DECISIONS
   - These are decisions I made that were good but not great.
   - If I had to do it all over again, I would improve something or change something. Upon evaluation, there are things I would do differently.
   - Wise leaders learn not only from their mistakes but from the outtakes of their decisions. Next time, I will...

3. STUPID DECISIONS
   - Just the dumbest thing I've ever done.
   - What were you thinking? The answer is, I wasn't.

4. SINFUL DECISIONS
   - Evil—They violate God's Word.

Leaders need to get some REST:

<u>R</u>estoring
<u>E</u>xperience designed to
<u>S</u>trengthen
<u>T</u>he mind, body, soul, and spirit (wholistic)

It's important to differentiate between rest that refreshes and rest that simply relieves. Seeking only relief is unhealthy in the long run.

Training Potential Leaders: (1 Timothy 3:8-10)

- TRAIN them. (vs. 9, must keep hold of the deep truths)
- TEST them. (vs. 10, must be tested)
- TRUST them. (Turn over and turn loose.) (vs. 10b, "and THEN if there is nothing... let them serve.")

Good Process in Mentoring:

- I do and you watch. (Model and teach.)
- I do and you do with me. (Do it together.)
- You do and I watch you. (Tune up and tweak.)
- You do and I do something else. (Turn over responsibility.)

Medical training model of "See one, do one, teach one."

3 Important Exercises for Leaders Regarding Their Values:

1. Evaluate your values.
   - What is important to your organization?
   - What are the non-negotiables?
   - Verify the DNA that you are absolutely committed to.

2. Value your values. (Hold them dear.)

3. Validate your values (by living them out).
   - Your values are your corporate or ministry culture.
     - Practice them.
     - Promote them.
     - Protect them.
     - Praise those who are implementing them.
   - When it comes to culture and values, actions speak louder than words.
   - The hypocrites of Jesus' day said one thing but did another. They didn't validate their values.
   - A mission statement is meaningless if you don't implement it.

As a Christian Leader, I am **COMMITTED** to:

Choosing God's ways rather than the ways of the world (Hebrews 11:25; Isaiah 55:8-9)

Obeying God and His Word in every area of my life (Acts 5:29; John 17:6)

Making the most of every opportunity for Christ (Ephesians 5:16; Colossians 4:5; Galatians 6:10)

Modeling Christ's example to those around me (1 Peter 2:21; 1 Timothy 4:12; 2 Thessalonians 3:6-13)

Integrity of Heart and Life (Psalm 25:21; Proverbs 10:9, 11:3)

Truth and Honesty (Ephesians 6:14; John 3:21)

Taming my Tongue (James 1:26, 3:5-9; 1 Peter 3:10)

Enlarging my borders (Growth) (1 Chronicles 4:10)

Decisions based on God's will, not my own (Proverbs 16:33; Matthew 26:39)

11 Biblical Guidelines for Setting Goals:

1. They must be measurable. (Luke 13:32)

2. They must be pleasing to God and according to His will. (2 Corinthians 5:9)

3. They must be large enough that they are totally dependent on God, not yourself. (Galatians 3:3)

4. They must be something we have not already obtained. (Philippians 4:12) In fact, they should be greater than what we have already obtained. (Philippians 4:16)

5. They must be something that has taken "hold" of us. (Philippians 3:12-13) When something has a hold on you, you cannot let it go.

6. They must be a priority. (Philippians 3:13, one thing)

7. They must be free from any baggage from the past. (Philippians 3:13)

8. They must be something we give a tremendous amount of energy and effort toward. (Philippians 3:13-14, straining and pressing)

9. They must be something we recruit others to help us accomplish. (Philippians 3:17)

10. They must be attempted with the right motives. (1 Timothy 1:5)

11. They must be a stretch of faith until they are accomplished. (1 Peter 1:9)

15 Scriptures Every Christian Leader Needs to be Reminded of from Time to Time:

1. You are responsible to God. (1 Corinthians 7:24; Romans 14:12)

2. You are serving God, not man. (Colossians 3:22-24)

3. A servant is not greater than his master. (Matthew 10:24-25)

4. You reap if you faint not. (Galatians 6:9)

5. Your reward is in Heaven (Matthew 5:11-12), not here. Remember, the rewards are greater later.

6. "Cast your burdens on the Lord for He cares for you" (1 Peter 5:7, NKJV).

7. "My grace is sufficient for you" (2 Cor. 12:9, NKJV).

8. The battle belongs to the Lord. (1 Samuel 17:47)

9. "Stand still and see the Salvation of the Lord" (Exodus 14:13, NKJV).

10. "God will supply all your needs" (Phil. 4:19, NKJV).

11. "Great is thy faithfulness" (Lam. 3:22-23, KJV).

12. "Without Me, you can do NOTHING" (Jn. 15:5, NKJV).

13. "With God, nothing is impossible" (Lk. 1:37, NKJV; Gen. 18:14, NKJV; Matt. 19:26, NKJV).

14. It's not by *our* might or by *our* spirit, but by *His*. (Zechariah 4:6)

15. I can do all things through Christ who gives me strength. (Philippians 4:13)

6 Load-bearing Problems in Leadership:

1. People who do not carry their own load (Galatians 6:5)
   - Team morale will eventually erode when team members do not carry their own load.
   - Either fire them up, or just fire them.

2. People who are too loaded down to be effective and efficient
   - When someone is too weighed down, their DO LIST will get delayed.

3. People who place too heavy a load on others (Luke 11:46)
   - Loads they expect from others but excuse in themselves. These leaders demand, discourage, damage, and defeat their followers with impossible loads.

4. People who try to carry the load all by themselves (Numbers 11:14)

5. People who don't rely on God to help them carry their load (Psalm 55:22-23; Matthew 11:28-30; Psalm 37:5)

6. People who don't divide up and delegate the load with others (Numbers 4)

"Written goals have a way of transforming wishes into wants, can'ts into cans, dreams into plans, and plans into reality. Don't just think it; ink it!" —unknown

"Thoughts disentangle themselves when they pass through the lips and fingertips." —Dawson Trotman

The goal trifecta: write it down, tell someone else, monitor progress.

6 Attributes of a Good Leader:

L = Listener
E = Empathic
A = Agile
D = Dedicated
E = Energetic
R = Reflective

5 Trust Builders:

T = Truthteller
R = Reliability
U = Understanding
S = Safety
T = Transparency

10 Keys to Dynamic LEADERSHIP:

<u>L</u>ongevity	Leaders persevere consistently over the long haul
<u>E</u>xample	Leaders set the expectation by walking their talk
<u>A</u>ppreciation	Leaders build spirit by taking the time to encourage
<u>D</u>reams	Leaders are continually daring to set new visions
<u>E</u>ducation	Leaders are continually daring to set new goals
<u>R</u>esponsibility	Leaders act and are accountable for their actions
<u>S</u>acrifice	Leaders give up to gain
<u>H</u>onesty	Leaders are truthful with themselves and those they lead
<u>I</u>nspiration	Leaders excite and equip others to get on board
<u>P</u>urpose	Leaders know where they are going and why

ACT—Developing a Plan:

<u>A</u>   Assess the situation (opportunities and challenges)

<u>C</u>   Connect with key players and collaborate on solutions

<u>T</u>   Tackle new ideas and innovation

4 Behaviors of a High-Performance Team:

    T = Trust
    E = Engagement
    A = Accountability
    M = Metrics

6 Types of Expectations:

1. Unknown (Expectations are not spoken until they are broken.)
2. Unproductive (NO expectations or set too LOW)
3. Unrealistic (Unrealistic expectations usually fall shy of their goal because they were set TOO HIGH.)
4. Unwritten
5. Unmet ("All disappointment is the result of unmet expectations." —Pat Morley)
6. Understood (These expectations are framed and followed because they are communicated and comprehended.)

When it comes to expectations, 4 things are necessary:

1. Set your expectations clearly.
2. Communicate your expectations.
3. Manage your expectations. (Check on them.)
4. Reward those who meet and exceed your expectations.

10 Clues to How Good Leaders Choose (Joshua 24:15)

1. What is best over what is good
2. Principle over what is popular
3. The greater good over what is good for me
4. Facts over feelings
5. Character over comfort
6. Integrity over special interest
7. What is good over what looks good
8. Commitment over convenience
9. Realistic over what is idealistic
10. Long-term solutions over a quick fix

12 Attributes to Attain and Retain in Leadership:

1. Humility (Proverbs 11:2; 15:33; 18:12)
2. Integrity (Proverbs 10:9; 20:7)
3. Wisdom (Proverbs 2:2, 10; 3:7)
4. Common sense (Proverbs 2:7; 13:15; 24:3)
5. Courage (Joshua 1:6-7,9,18)
6. Reliability (Proverbs 12:22; 13:17; 20:6)
7. Kindness (Proverbs 3:3; 11:17)
8. Resilience (James 1:2-4)
9. Honesty (Proverbs 11:3,5)
10. Patience (Proverbs 16:32; 25:15)
11. Self-Control (Proverbs 16:32; 25:28)
12. Hard-working (Proverbs 12:24; 13:14)

Leadership is:

1. INTEGRITY. Image is who people think we are; integrity is who we really are. Leadership is built on TRUST. People will not follow someone they cannot trust. Leadership consists of character and strategy. If you can't have both, opt for character.

2. INFLUENCE. The classic definition of leadership: leadership is influence. Leaders don't only impact others; they influence them for the good. The key to successful leadership today is influence, not authority.

3. INNOVATION. New wine for new wine skins. For the church to remain effective in the 21st century, our leaders must make creativity and technology part of our way of thinking. (Color outside the lines.) We must spend more time reflecting, refining, and risking.

4. INTERACTION. You manage things and lead people. To lead people effectively, you need to interact with them. Love and listen and appreciate the people who are following you, or you will soon be left alone. Leaders must be close enough to relate to others but far enough ahead to motivate them.

5. INSPIRATION. Leadership is fueled by God-given, man-motivating vision. A leader must be hearing from God, casting the vision, and leading the way.

6. INQUISITIVE. Leaders ask questions; they want to know more. Leaders are readers. When you stop learning, you stop leading. Leaders seek continual improvement.

7. INITIATIVE. Vision without action is just a dream. Leadership is figuring out what needs to be done and then doing it. Be a self-starter.

8. INTUITION. Leadership is not a science; it is an art. It is that inner voice that is learned through success and failure.

9. INTERDEPENDENT. Leadership is WE. Effective leadership is built on teams. Transforming leadership is not based on one person who holds a title but on a team who has talent.

10. INSTRUCTIVE. "Success without a successor is failure." —John C. Maxwell. The power of leadership is in multiplication. Everyone needs a Paul and a Timothy in their life. We must be looking to reproduce ourselves in leadership.

Leaders will subtract anything that is:

1. Distractive
2. Unproductive
3. Counterproductive
4. Obstructive (Preventing movement)
5. Addictive
6. Competitive
7. Disruptive
8. Destructive
9. Ineffective

10 Warning Signs that Hardship Has Hardened a Leader:

2. Passive instead of passionate
3. Indifferent instead of intentional
4. Resistant instead of resilient
5. Careless instead of cautious
6. Reactionary instead of reflective
7. Indecisive instead of intuitive
8. Discouraging instead of discerning
9. Calloused instead of conscientious
10. Overwhelmed instead of ability to overcome
11. Critical and cynical instead of complimentary

A Lesson on Leaving—

Don't leave:

- Without completing your portion of the mission, if possible
  - Do what you were called to do and came to do.
  - As much as it depends on you, get it done before you're done.
  - Make sure there is no unfinished business.

- Without navigating through a season of crisis
  - Financial
  - Relational
  - Organizational
  - National

- Without doing your part to resolve any relational conflict (Romans 12:18)

- Without eliminating any cloud of controversy or accusation
  - Work through it before you are through.

- Without leaving things better than when you came
  - Leave a positive impact.
  - Leave a legacy, not a catastrophe.

- Without mentoring and training those left behind to lead
    - Transition your team for future success in your absence.

- Without clear direction and confirmation from God

- Without finishing well. (2 Timothy 4:7)
    - Take the high road on the route out.
    - Land the plane without incident or accident.

The success or failure of any leader often boils down to how they made choices.

- Choice leaders make great choices
- Leaders don't stand a chance of success without making great choices
- A leader cannot afford to leave their choices to chance.

My Personal Leadership Values

These are things I value and desire to intentionally and consistently put into practice in my personal leadership:

I want Christ to be at center stage in my life and leadership, and I want to share the rest of the stage with people God has placed in my life to help me lead.

I want to always give God glory for everything and share the credit with those on my team who help make it happen.

I want to be dependent on God for every step I take and in everything I do. (2 Corinthians 1:9; 2 Corinthians 3:5)

I want to be humble and have a servant's heart in my leadership role.

I want to lead myself and others well. I want to never stop growing, learning, and gaining in understanding and wisdom.

I want to be intentional about being relational.

I want to be firm in my beliefs but flexible in my strategy.

I want to be thankful and show that appreciation through tangible expressions of gratitude to others.

I want to be as personal, relational, and approachable as possible in my approach to connecting with people.

I want to always be fully prepared for every opportunity that comes my way. I don't want to ever short-change my preparation based on the size or significance of the opportunity.

I want to be willing to be stretched in my thinking and keep an open mind to ideas that are different, or even contrary, to mine.

I want to be creative and innovative in my approach to leadership and the challenges and changes that come my way.

I want to invest my life in people who are hungry, faithful, available, teachable, and leadable.

I want to be willing to do what is right or what is best for the group over what is popular. (Galatians 1:10; Acts 5:29)

I want to be known as someone who is EARLY in everything I do. I like to meet or beat deadlines EVERY TIME. I want things to be on time, stay on time, and end on time.

I want to be organized and develop organizational systems and structure for making sure tasks do not fall through the cracks.

I want to be caring and candid with the people around me. I want to be gentle but truthful and firm, full of grace, and full of truth. (John 1:14)

I want to never stop growing, learning, and evaluating in my personal life and in my ministry setting.

I want to be consistent and constant in my example to others. I want to develop a reputation in any leadership setting of someone who is carefully consistent in what he does.

I want to look for opportunities every day to encourage someone in their life's journey.

I want to always be looking forward to what's coming and following up with things after they have taken place.

I want to be intentional about what I do and don't do and why I do or don't do it.

I want to be approachable and always be willing to stop what I'm doing and focus my attention on the person who has approached me.

I want to take responsibility for everything that happens under my leadership watch. I don't want to pass the buck or throw someone else under the bus.

I want to always leave a leadership assignment or task with which I've been entrusted in better shape when I'm finished than when I took ownership of it.

I want to be missional in life. I want to lead others to be outward-focused more than inward-centered.

I want to take advantage of every opportunity God brings into my path and commit to carrying it out with excellence.

I want to be in constant pursuit of improvement

I want to have fun and enjoy the journey of life and leadership.

I want to FINISH WELL. (2 Timothy 4:7; Philemon 2:16)

Board Governance

3 Seats Where Executives Sit on a Governing Board:

1. The CEO serves as the authority. (He/she is the voice and the vote. The board is a "yes board" and does exactly what the leader wants. There is almost zero accountability.

2. The CEO serves as the minority. (He/she serves as an employee, the one member of the board who does not get a vote. He/she gets a voice but no vote.

3. The CEO serves as a priority but is governed by the majority. He/she is the first among equals. (CEO gets a voice AND a vote.)

Numbers 1 and 2 are problematic in governance.

BOARDS focus on:

Big picture
- Remain in their lane
- Macro vs. micro

Oversight and observation
- Organizational health and excellence
- Financial matters (Ensure transparency.)
- Governance

- The President/CEO (the only employee we oversee)
- Compliance issues (organization constitution and legal matters)
- Protection against potential danger (1 Timothy 6:20; Proverbs 22:3, 27:12)
- Itself (Great boards govern themselves.)
- The vision and strategic plan

Advising and advancing the mission of the organization
- Offering opinion on best course of action
- The leadership of the organization
- Sharing wisdom and insight
- Asking great questions.

Receive reports and resolve issues
- Boards receive information and give input on innovation.
- This is where committees can play a key role. (Save time in board meetings.)

Deliberation and decision making
- While committees do a lot of leg work, ultimate decisions are made by the board. (They review and recommend, but the board determines.)
- Board reports should drive board discussion and decisions.

Setting policy and direction

- Board Member Expectations:

    o To be a positive ambassador, adviser, and advocate for the board and organization

    o Attend all regularly scheduled board meetings as well as participate in any conference calls or video meetings that take place outside the regularly scheduled meetings.
      - The next 3 meetings should be established by the end of each official meeting.

    o Read all monthly reports and information sent to the board.
      - Respond with any appropriate feedback or follow up.
      - Reply to any board action in a timely manner (things that require a vote).

    o To stay informed regarding the organization, its ministries, its issues, and its opportunities.

    o Prepare and pray for all meetings in advance. Boards have a distinct advantage when their members are prayerfully prepared in advance for meetings.

    o To help create and maintain a healthy board culture of trust, empowerment, and positive engagement.

- — Healthy boards govern themselves.
- — Effective board meetings depend on developing a healthy board culture. A board's culture refers to its beliefs, values, attitudes, and customs.
- — The fact that the board has fiduciary responsibilities does not require the board to refrain from any form of fun or enjoyment.

o To value and respect opposing viewpoints. We need to leave room for diversity of thought.

o To help ensure the board functions in compliance with the organization's constitution and all standing policies of the board.

o To help evaluate board meetings, board policy, and board engagement.

o To maintain confidentiality in all internal matters of board and organizational importance.
   - — Confidentiality is critical in leadership and for the success of the board.

o To keep your focus and attention on the big picture and helping to advance the mission.

o To sign an annual conflict of interest disclosure and update it during the year, if necessary, as well as disclose potential conflicts before meetings and actual conflicts during meetings.

- o To advise, communicate, encourage, and pray for the leadership of the organization.
  - — The board governs, and has but one agent, the President/CEO, who hires all other staff.
  - — As board members, we are directly responsible for one employee, the president of the organization. It is our job to pray for and come alongside the president with all means of support, encouragement, assistance, and accountability.
- o To adhere to the limitations of the board, its committees, and individual board members.
- o To allow the Spirit to guide all matters of conversation, direction, and decisions.

- Board meeting expectations:
  - o To arrive on time, ready to engage when the meeting begins.
  - o To stay for the duration of the scheduled board meeting, when possible.
    - — There will be circumstances from time to time that make this impossible.

- o To stay fully engaged for the duration of the meeting.
- o To actively engage in board meeting discussions.
  - — As a board member, you not only have a vote but also a voice.
  - — It is important for each individual board member to give input in the discussion and then fully support the decision once it has been made.
  - — Interacting and inserting your insight
  - — Sharing your thoughts, creative ideas, and concerns
  - — Giving your honest feedback and perspective.
  - — Weighing in with your opinions
  - — Asking challenging questions. (Challenge the process.)
- o To speak your own opinion during the discussion stage but fully support what the entire board determines to be the final decision.
  - — All matters of discussion should be handled in a manner of respect with a goal of diversity of ideas, thought, and opinion.
- o To carry out specific assignments or duties delegated by the board during its session.

- o To help the board stay on task in terms of agenda and responsibilities.

- Board Governance:
  - o The board should hold helpful discussions and then move toward a decision.
  - o The board has a responsibility to review and ratify recommendations of the president, directors, and committees. To ratify does not mean to retry an entire decision.
  - o The only reason to abstain from a vote is conflict of interest. Otherwise, "let your yes be yes and your no be no." (Matthew 5:37)
  - o The board has the power to set policy, procedure, and practice but must first walk it through the proper path of approval.
  - o Note that when the board is in executive session, it has the authority only to deal with matters regarding the president and his office. Discussions and decisions regarding all other matters should be held until the full board is in session.

12 Suggestions for "Improving Your Serve" in Board Leadership:

1. Refrain from serving on any board for the sole purpose of personal gain.

2. Follow Jesus' example who came to serve, not to be served.
   - Remember that you do not sit in a position of leadership for the personal perks. Position yourself to serve.
   - Too many leaders sign on to boards for what they can get, not what they can give.

2. Be intentional to use your leadership gift as a lift to the organization you oversee. Exercise your expertise.

3. Educate yourself in the environment where you have a platform for leadership.

4. Focus more on asking the right questions than giving the right answers.
   - Then listen, learn, lead!
   - It is a limited understanding of the important function of a board member if you think your role is to give the right answers.

- It is essential that board members are probing the issues through presenting proper questions.

5. Never fail to give appropriate feedback.
   - Organizational leaders appreciate appropriate feedback from board members. A lack of feedback can be a real setback on any board
   - You don't have to write an essay to say something significant. Something practical can be profound. One of the key roles of a board member is to respond in a timely manner.
   - A good board member will comment on the content of board reports.

6. Advance the mission of the organization by preparing for each meeting in advance.
   - Preparation is the best predictor of productivity.
   - The staff has an obligation to properly prepare for each board meeting.
   - A chain is only as strong as its weakest link.
   - A board member has an obligation to come to meetings prepared to engage.
   - Read reports and highlight points of discussion and clarification.
   - Get a handle on important issues.

- Access the agenda in advance.
- Jot down ideas, insights, issues, or information you feel should be addressed or further explained.
  - Too many board members treat their board service like they do their camper when they go on a trip. They hook up when they pull into the park, turn on the water and electricity, and enjoy the experience, but turn it all off and pack it all up when they pull out of the park. They don't touch it until they go again.

7. Keep a record of assigned tasks to complete before the next meeting.

8. Police the jurisdiction you have been elected and entrusted to govern by getting a decent grip on your organizational policies.

9. Be an advocate for the administration.

10. Introduce the organization to the influential people you interact with.

11. Don't derail a discussion with too many details.
    - Avoid any possibility of a "discussion concussion" or analysis paralysis.
    - It's possible to respond without repeating.

12. Put more sensation in your presentation.
   - Sensation is a feeling of excitement and heightened interest.
   - Just because you sit on a board doesn't mean you have to make everyone else bored when you speak.
   - Put more planning into your presentations.

"Now That's a Great QUESTION!":

They say boards should be composed of individuals who bring one or more of these three qualities to the table: work, wealth, and/or wisdom.

When it comes to board wisdom, leaders are sometimes intimidated and misguided concerning their role of bringing wisdom into the board room. They assume a good board member provides intelligent answers. The reality is, great board members facilitate the right answer by asking the right questions.

Board leadership is not as much about knowing the right answers as knowing what the right questions are to ask and when to ask them.

Successful boards ask better questions; as a result, they acquire better answers.

6 Types of Questions that Might Move Boards in the Right Direction:

1. Clarifying questions (to make more comprehensible)
   - More information or more details are necessary to be fully informed.
     - Might look like, "Can you help me understand..." or "Explain..."
   - These types of questions bring clarity to a proposal or presentation. They help us understand what is unclear.
   - Often the presenter is so present (so comfortable) concerning the subject that necessary details might remain absent to the board.
   - Clarifying questions help us discover content and context.
   - Clarifying questions will verify information.

2. Identifying questions
   - Details that help prevent possible pitfalls, shortfalls, and downfalls
   - Investigative questions: who, what, when, where, why, and how
   - These questions help identify next steps in the process of approval, implementation, and follow-up.

3. Qualifying questions (to fulfill a necessary condition)
   - These are questions that press the eligibility of an idea making sure it reaches the certain standard of the organization's vision and values.
     o Does it fit with our purpose, mission, and vision?
     o Not every great idea should be implemented.
     o Is this a good idea that would divert us from our primary purpose?
     o There will always be more good ideas than we have capacity to execute.
   - These are alignment questions.
   - Qualifying questions ensure the standard of excellence set by leadership, the meeting and exceeding of expectations.
   - Qualifying questions often merge into quantifying questions (data details, budget details, and timing details).
   - Boards must be careful not to get stuck in the weeds. They can easily be distracted from the big picture oversight/direction of the organization.

4. Modifying questions
   - These are questions that might suggest a slight change in the original proposal on the table.

- They may lead us to a discovery on an alternate route that would be more beneficial.
  - "Would it be better if we...."
  - "What if we..."
- These questions inspire improvement and innovation of the original idea.
- It is through these modifying moments (questions) that good ideas become great ideas.
- Modifying questions typically emerge and evolve into magnifying questions: "How can we enlarge this idea into something bigger and better?"
- Can it be said after your board meeting that an idea got better?

5. Ratifying questions
   - These questions move from improving to approving the idea or concept. They may even require changes to organizational policy, procedure, or practice.
     - The difference between modifying and ratifying is that in modifying, you make slight changes to make the idea better. In ratifying, you make changes in policy or procedure to make the idea possible.

- The approval of a proposal and documentation of that decision and moving forward
- A course is outlined of implementation and inspection (follow-up and review).
- An action item goes from paper, to process, to progress.

6. Implementing questions.
   - These questions deal with next steps and how we will measure success. Who will lead the charge?
   - Who has authority to lead, and who will be accountable for the decision?
   - How will we evaluate the project?
   - What kind of resources will be needed?

What I've discovered is that thought-provoking questions take preparation.

Great thought-out questions lead to great discussion; great discussions lead to great discoveries; and great discoveries ultimately lead to great decisions. Better decisions more effectively direct our organizations to their desired goals and preferred picture of the future.

Eric Schmidt, CEO of Google from 2001-2011, said, "We run this company on questions, not on answers."

Some Final "Q" Tips (Question Tips) for Your Next Board Meeting:

1. Prepare your questions in advance to bring to the board table.
   - Questions are unquestionably better when they are thought out in advance. Just as a good answer is well thought out, so is a good question.
   - Take some time to write down your questions.
   - If you really want to take it to the next level, after reading a board report, email the right person and ask your question in advance.

2. Remember, it may be more appropriate to ask some questions privately than with everyone.
   - Your question need not involve everyone in the room if it does not impact everyone in the room.
   - There is typically a lot of time wasted in board meetings because of this.
   - Be careful that you don't default to this and deprive everyone of important information and discussion.

3. Keep your questions designed as questions, not answers disguised as questions.
   - One of the hardest things in coaching is to ask questions and not state advice as a question.
   - You nullify a question when it does not classify as a question.

4. Keep in mind that great questions should challenge the process, not a person.
   - Sometimes you must give attention to tension in the room (personality conflicts).

5. Carefully consider the intensity of the question as well as the quality of the question. A great question can sometimes get derailed by the perception of the tone or body language. Your tone can cause a lot of trouble.
   - An appropriate topic to question can be toxic if it is done in the wrong way or at the wrong time.

6. Tough questions can combust in the absence of trust.
   - Once significant relationship is established between members of the board and trust is formed, it is much easier to ask difficult questions because of the relational trust that

is present, and a motive is not being questioned.

7. Not all great questions can be or should be answered immediately; some may need to be pondered and pursued.
   - A great question will often linger and take the board on a journey of discovery. You don't have to rush to respond. Sometimes you may need to research before you respond.

8. Don't let an immediate pause in questions be the cause of a terminated discussion.
   - Often a great discussion is shut down a second away from a breakthrough.

9. Refrain from asking a question that does not pertain to the discussion at hand.
   - Keep it and ask it later. Don't derail a conversation with a question that does not apply.
   - Questions that lead down rabbit trails can hijack a meeting.

10. Take time to fully listen to a question before you attempt to enlighten with an answer.
    - Make sure you understand the question before you answer it.
    - Sometimes the most appropriate answer is another question.

- Ken Coleman said, "Good questions inform; great questions transform."

What kind of questions are you prepared to ask in your meeting?

When you ask a question:
- Don't assume
- Don't accuse
- Don't attack
- Don't abandon
...the topic by diverting to a completely unrelated discussion until the one at hand is discussed.

"The art of proposing a question must be held of higher value than solving it." —Georg Cantor

Peter Drucker said, "The most serious mistakes are not being made as a result of wrong answers. The true dangerous thing is asking the wrong questions."

"People who enjoy meetings should not be in charge of anything." —Thomas Sowell

Board Frustrations from the Perspective of the CEO:

1. When the board is proceeding through a meeting without proper preparation. Reports are received but not read.

2. When there is a lack of adequate feedback
    - Tell your board members why they need to reply and how.

3. When discussions are derailed because of too many details
    - Discussions can get detailed to death.

4. When there is silence during the discussion stage and chatter after the matter is decided

5. When board members serve without volunteering
    - Remember the 3 hats board members wear (TheAndringaGroup.com)
      - Governance
      - Implementation
      - Volunteer

6. When there is deliberation without consideration for those who will be most impacted by the decision
    - Decisions are often implemented without the input of those closest to the situation.

7. When there are decisions that are finalized without a formalized plan of action (determination without implementation)
   - There needs to be a plan in place to tailgate what you delegate.

8. When there is a lack of confidence in the confidentiality of the board (information leaks)
   - What happens in Vegas doesn't stay in Vegas.

9. When there is an illusion that we may be reaching a conclusion
   - Looks like we are going to make a decision, then it disappears
   - We regress our progress, then go on and on.

10. When the board regularly revisits already-reached conclusions.
    - We keep rewinding and rehashing.
    - 3 steps forward, 3 steps back
    - Many board meetings resemble Groundhog Day.

11. When we rush a vote on an issue without the opportunity to first reach unity on the idea
    - Because it was pushed, the motion passed, but so did the momentum.

- Sometimes the best thing we can do on a board is wait and pray for God to unify us.

12. When the passion for the mission is only present at the meeting
   - When enthusiasm fades following the meeting

13. Members who don't understand their role on the board or the rules that govern the board

14. When board reports are not relevant

15. When board vacancies are filled with good people who are not good leaders

16. When leaders govern but don't give to the organization

17. When boards process information without making progress

18. When problems are recognized but progress is not
   - When they spend disproportionate time on what's wrong instead of what's right

19. When board members are present but don't participate

20. When little attention is given to regular board attendance

Questions for Coaching Leaders:

1. What resources are you reading that are making you a stronger leader?

2. What are you learning from observing other leaders?

3. How are you developing and improving your leadership strengths?

4. What's weighing on you that is impacting your work?

5. How are you reserving time for resting, relaxing, and refreshing?

6. Are there leadership challenges you are procrastinating rather than processing? What obstacle is standing in the way of overcoming the challenge?

7. Who are you collaborating with for the purpose of elaborating on a creative idea?

8. Is there anything you should be examining more deeply that you are currently overlooking or excusing?

9. What tasks are you focused on completing in the immediate future? What added input would impact the outcome?

10. How are you intentionally investing your time mentoring future leaders?

11. What ongoing practices encourage you to grow as a leader?

12. Are there competing priorities and practices you should consider eliminating to create space for success? What are they?

13. As you move toward excellence, what specific things need improving?

14. Is there anything tempting you that could destroy your character and should be tempered?

15. Who are you regularly consulting with who inspires creative solutions?

16. How are you ranking priorities in your life?

17. How are you envisioning your future? How can you implement your intent? What will it take to accomplish something great?

18. How are you serving those you are leading?

19. What are you experiencing that you find encouraging?

34 Scriptures to Help You BE a Better Leader

BE fruitful and multiply.	Genesis 1:22, 28; 9:1, 7
BE strong and courageous.	Joshua 1:6; 1 Corinthians 16:13; Ephesians 6:10
BE acceptable.	Psalm 19:14; James 1:26
BE a witness.	Acts 1:8
BE transformed.	Romans 12:2
BE without hypocrisy.	Romans 12:9
BE devoted.	Romans 12:10; Matthew 6:4
BE of the same mind.	Romans 12:16; 2 Corinthians 13:4
BE subject.	Romans 13:1, 5
BE renewed.	Ephesians 4:23
BE angry and sin not.	Ephesians 4:26
BE kind to one another.	Ephesians 4:32

BE imitators of God.	Ephesians 5:1
BE careful how you walk.	Ephesians 5:15, 16
BE filled with the Spirit.	Ephesians 5:18
BE obedient.	Ephesians 6:5
BE humble.	Philippians 2:3; Ephesians 4:2
BE anxious for nothing.	Philippians 4:6
BE content.	Philippians 4:11
BE above reproach.	1 Timothy 3:2
BE diligent.	2 Timothy 2:15
BE ready.	2 Timothy 4:2
BE sober.	2 Timothy 4:5; 1 Peter 5:8
BE quick.	James 1:19
BE patient.	James 5:7, 8
BE holy.	1 Peter 1:15, 16
BE submissive.	1 Peter 2:18

BE of sound judgment.	1 Peter 4:7
BE hospitable.	1 Peter 4:9
BE subject.	1 Peter 5:5
BE alert.	1 Peter 5:8, 9; Ephesians 6:18, 19
BE on guard.	2 Peter 1:10, 15; 3:14
BE faithful.	Revelation 2:10; 1 Corinthians 4:2

About the Author

Bert Jones serves as director of leadership and church relations for Christian Medical & Dental Associations (CMDA) in Bristol, Tennessee. In this role, Bert oversees the Center for Well-being. He also serves as chaplain of CMDA. Bert spends his time traveling, preaching, speaking, writing, training, and coaching.

Since 1988, Bert has led multiple teams across the street and around the world, traveling to more than thirty countries on five different continents to teach and preach the gospel. He has engaged in leadership development nationally and internationally throughout his ministry.

Bert co-authored the book *Servant Leadership Proverbs* in 2017 with Dr. David Stevens, published by CMDA. Prior to that project, Dr. Stevens and Bert co-authored the book *Leadership Proverbs,* published by CMDA as well.

Prior to rejoining the staff of CMDA, Bert served as senior pastor of Woodburn Missionary Church and as president and CEO of GO InterNational.

Bert and his wife, Cheryl, have been married since 1989 and have three children—Joshua (married to Kali), Allyson, and Aaron—and one grandson, named Judah.

Bert serves as moderator for the General Oversight Council of Missionary Church USA, on the board of directors of GO InterNational, and chairs the board of directors of Pathways Pregnancy Resource Center in Bristol, Tennessee.

Christian Medical & Dental Associations (CMDA) exists to educate, encourage, and equip Christian healthcare professionals to glorify God. Founded in 1931, CMDA is the largest community of Christian healthcare professionals and students in the world whose purpose is to change hearts in healthcare. CMDA continues to minister on a majority of medical and dental school campuses, trains students and graduates in leadership skills for effective practice and ministry, provides regional and national conferences for fellowship and education and provides opportunities for short-term mission trips as well as international academic and clinical teaching opportunities. CMDA also serves as a voice of its members to the media, churches and government by speaking out on bioethical, health, and human rights issues. For more information and to become a member, visit *www.cmda.org.*

Christian
Medical & Dental
Associations®
Changing Hearts in Healthcare